"In a malleable world where everything from
atoms to cells is changing to match our beliefs,
we're limited only by the way we think of
ourselves in that world."

— Gregg Braden

"You have the power to heal your life, and you
need to know that. We think so often that we
are helpless, but we're not. We always have the
power of our minds... Claim and consciously use
your power."

— Louise Hay

THE
EMPOWERED
EMPATH
PROGRAM

From Anxious to
Empowered in 9 Weeks

ISBN: 979-8-985607-81-9 (eBook)
ISBN: 979-8-9856078-2-6 (paperback)

Published in the United States.

To all who served as my most precious teachers in life, whether you know your impact or not, you taught me well.

A NOTE OF THANKS

Many thanks go to all my clients who continually trust me with their energy, innermost secrets and relentlessly cheer on my work. To my online followers who comprise a loving network and intentional community that is safe for all in a world with few truly safe spaces.

CONTENTS

INTRODUCTION

This book is intended to speak to your soul on a deep and resonant level. It is also true that this book lobbies to your identity; who you are, the way you think about yourself, the way you are viewed by the world and the characteristics that define you. All of this influences the way in which you move through this world and how you emanate your soul expression. It has a lot to do with your "I AM" presence.

You will notice a theme through out the chapter titles in the book. There is a focus on the "I". This is because by looking inwardly at self, you able to connect, relate, share, impact and influence the world around you in the most clear and aligned manner possible. To put it simply, you are much more powerful.

When you are in touch and in tune with your heart and soul's truth on a foundational level, there is literally nothing you cannot achieve.

There is a reason you felt called to pick up this book. I'm not in the business of deciding what that reason is, since personal choices are exactly that; personal. However, I've had the honor of working with thousands of clients over the years helping them to find the personal power within and let their beautiful god-given light shine out into this world. Through providing one-on-one readings, offering energy sessions, teaching classes, giving interviews and creating videos and content online, I've been granted the opportunity to work with individuals from all walks of life.

I could share story after story where I've witnessed clients do miraculous feats in their own lives just by developing the empathic gifts that are already intrinsically there. Lives have been changed, life long health issues have been resolved, true love has been found, families have been created, dream careers have been cultivated, financial abundance has been received, life long goals achieved. To say developing your empathic abilities is powerful is an understatement.

However, it's due to my own personal experiences that I trust it will benefit your life immensely, if not change it completely for the better. Aside from gifting me with a life and career that I'm absolutely in love with, it has saved my life on multiple occasions.

By healing yourself, you're revealing yourself and will no doubt end up falling in love with yourself.

I am driven to bring Empath Education to the masses. It's not your fault that you have needed to seek out information on how to tap into your own energy. They don't teach these crucial life skills in your average school, yet they are so very necessary for the sensitive soul. More and more sensitive souls are being born with every passing generation as the world moves through a mass awakening to subtle levels of consciousness.

You may be one of these precious souls who were born with "the lights on". If that's the case, my deepest respect for you.

I felt very much aware of unseen things that others couldn't "see" since birth, and I tell ya, it's a hard way to go. To be the only one in the room who can feel energy or is aware of beings in other dimensions can make for a very lonely childhood.

By working with so many empaths, starseeds, earth angels, light workers and wayshowers in my personal practice, I've had the privilege of channeling the Higher selves of these gifted souls. By bringing a deeper understanding of how these gifts work and where they can be practically applied in the physical realm will literally change the collective evolution of consciousness, as well as your life.

This is information for the New Earth.

PART 1

THE

APPROACH

What is the Difference between an HSP (Highly Sensitive Person), Starseed, Earth Angel, Light Worker and Empath?

In my opinion, it all depends on who you ask. A therapist may label you as an HSP, while a psychiatrist may identify you as introverted or INFJ (Introversion, Intuition, Feeling and Judgement on the Meyers-Briggs personality test). An energy healer may look at you and see you as an earth angel or light worker based on your soul agreements and work in this life. If you feel particularly drawn to all things cosmic and galactic in nature, or discover soul origin in other star systems, you may also resonate with the term Starseed. But I believe the term empath can be an all-encompassing term that is applied across the board when you are a sensitive soul.

That's the thing with labels, you decide which one you want to wear, if any. For the intents and purposes of discussing energy management and development through out this program, we will go with the term empath for now.

The term empath is a fairly recent one that many sensitive souls connect and relate to. It is my goal to walk you, the reader, through a step-by-step process of uncovering your own natural psychic abilities, empathic sensitivities and innate soul gifts so you can shine your unique and innovative light upon the world!

IDENTIFY WHAT'S COVERED

The goal with this book is to take you on a journey within the realms of your own consciousness. By tapping into your own innate gifts and abilities, you are able to unlock inherent power to transform anything in your reality.

If you are looking for scientific research and evidence based references, this is not the book for you. This book is written purely from first hand experience and joyfully tapping into the conscious stream of unconditional love. This book is not meant to satiate your logical mind lobbying for rationale and justifications. This book is meant to speak directly to your soul.

As you progress through the weeks, you will go on a journey from anxiety city, overwhelm ocean and stuck station to travel all the way to the magical land of healing, empowerment and freedom! Be aware, this is no quick fix. There is no magic pill that can change your life without you putting in some of the energetic motor behind the transformation.

Begin your journey now by saying to yourself out loud:

"I AM AN EMPOWERED EMPATH!!"

Claim it!

By the end of this book, you will have no doubt in your mind or hesitation within your energy that this statement is absolutely true.

Reading this book and progressing through the program of self exploration, will not only illuminate why developing your empathy skills are important, but it also gives you understanding, as well as the tools, to begin changing your life for the better right now.

We are all pre-wired with the ability to connect to Divine Source, cosmic consciousness, the All-That-Is. You are like a radio antenna that can pick up and tap into energy frequencies simply by being you! Although some of us are a bit more sensitive and fine-tuned to the subtleties of energy and the human experience, by design, we all need to continually return to Source energy, like a radio antenna would need a power source.

Even a Breatharian like the famous Ray Maor has learned that even though he can survive without food and water, he can only do so by remaining connected to universal source energy.

Unfortunately there are a lot of conditions and programs that have been running in this world, culture and society that are designed to push you into a state of fear, disconnecting your from your source of power. A person in fear is a person easily controlled, disempowered, and a person who has forgotten who they truly are.

> *"Fearful people are more dependent, more easily manipulated and controlled, more susceptible to deceptively simple, strong, tough measures and hard-line postures. They may accept and even*

welcome repression if it promises to relieve their insecurities."
— G e o r g e   G e r b n e r

When you live in fear and illusion, when you take action that is out of alignment with who you truly are, it separates you from that connection to Divine Love. This can result in mental illness, anxiety, disease, physical maladies, toxic situations, unhealthy environments, unequal relationships, dependancies, financial issues, lack of direction, loneliness, and the list goes on.

When you live in fear, you tend to believe that it is all up to you. Hoarding may become a habit. Whether it be hoarding food, emotions, money, old and stagnant energy, it doesn't matter. When you hold on to things because you "may need it later," that sends a message to the Universe that you don't believe that you will have enough, be enough, or you won't have what you need when you need it. That shifts your whole mindset into a self-centered, defensive mentality that is dislocated from Source.

When you rely solely on the ego self to bring in what you need, that is where the overwhelm comes in. That is when you become anxious and fearful.

"Oh no, we won't have enough food to eat if there's a natural disaster. Let's stockpile food in the garage and watch it expire."

"I don't have any time for myself because I have to hustle all day, everyday just to make rent. I'm the only one bringing in the money, it's all up to me."

"This person may not be my one true love but they are good enough and I'm never letting them go! We will be together forever!"

When you cling to these things, it is through your thoughts and actions that you clearly state to the Universe:

"I fear this may never come along again, so I'm going to attach to this."

Ultimately, what that does is it leaves zero room for any other miracles to happen. A message of divine guidance or a blessing that could change your life for the better may want to come along, but it sees you're already occupied and have your walls up, so the things that may be better for you, further in alignment, will pass you by.

This book is written from the prospective of Divine Universal Love. It does not subscribe to any religious pretext or undertone. Whether you already have a strong faith and devout practice or you have struggled with trusting the Love of the Universe, this book simply reconnects you to the power source that you already have within.

By reading this book and progressing through the program, you are opening up and making the space to embrace your natural gifts and abilities, and then expand on them. You are entering into relationship with Divine Source, Unconditional Love. You are healing, revealing and falling in love with yourself. You are shifting major energy and making room for the miracles to pour in today!

HOW TO USE THIS BOOK

There is no right or wrong way to learn. You know how you digest information better than anyone. With that being said, I will recommend how to move through this program.

It is a lot of information to take in all in one go. I recommend approaching it chapter by chapter or week by week as it is labeled. Reading and implementing the practices and activities one week at a time.

Although the information is broken down into weeks, please feel welcome to take more time if desired to really marinate in and absorb what you are learning. This will allow you time to fully integrate any new changes you are making as a result of reading the book since these energy shifts will certainly affect all aspects of your life; mood, creativity, relationships, work, even your sleep may change as a result!

There are a number of activities shared each week through out this book that I highly encourage you to try. You may feel silly doing them at first or not feel they are important, yet I would argue that they are necessary in order for you to really know what's possible within you.

There are many places for you to write in this book, such as in activities or after proposed questions. I really want you to feel free to write all over this book. Highlight sections. Draw doodles in the margins. Make notes about random things that pop in your mind while reading. You can even keep a journal alongside you while reading this book. Really let yourself get creative and feel free to explore and express what is coming through you.

The purpose of these exercises is to direct your focus to specific places that connect you with energy streams and potentials within your own energy. It's one thing for me to tell you how cool it is to be an empath but it's a whole other thing for you to experience it for yourself. For example, I can tell you all day long what a blueberry tastes like. But if you've never tasted a blueberry for yourself, you simply won't know the full experience.

RESULTS FROM
READING THIS BOOK

Upon completion of this program, you will have a better understanding of your emotional, mental, physical and energy bodies, allowing you to move through the world in full alignment. Rather than being bombarded and inundated with information that leaves you feeling (at best) confused by paranormal phenomenon and (at worst) paralyzed with fear and stuck in an existence filled with suffering, you will have all the tools at your disposal to keep you standing firm in your personal power, no matter the circumstance.

Developing your gifts of empathy will positively enhance your entire life. This may sound like a bold claim, but learning about and loving yourself truly changes your life for the better. It may lead to:

- Better connection and understanding of your body, thought patterns and emotions
- Discovering hidden psychic gifts and abilities
- The ability to stay flexible and adapt to changing conditions outside of your control
- Healing physical conditions and ailments
- Finding or creating the job of your dreams

- Healthy and fulfilling relationships
- Manifesting a life partner
- Helping animals or humanity in a truly impactful way
- Creating precious art or bodies of work
- Living your dream life
- Maintaining peace and harmony through out all areas of your life

And that is just to name a few possibilities that come from doing the inner work of developing yourself as an empath!

Just keep in mind, how fast you benefit from this book depends entirely on you and your own personal pace of development and evolution. You won't see such major results unless you implement these practices into your daily life and truly integrate what you discover.

In order to get the most out of this book, you need to remain open. Trust yourself and trust the process. Everyone has a different life path, as well as set of gifts and abilities. There will be some information in here that does not apply to you. My advice: if something resonates with you, take it. If something does not resonate with you, leave it alone.

If some concepts or activities seem really out there to you, play along and act as if, in the beginning. This will help you to suspend one of the biggest hurtles in developing psychic abilities: self-doubt.

Many of us get accustomed to living with self-doubt. We just invite it into the passenger seat to go on the journey with us. For this journey, that won't work. You need to kick self-doubt out of the vehicle as soon as you can. You *must* trust yourself first.

Your life *will* change. I won't claim that this book will change your life. But I will claim, after reading this book, *YOU* will change your life.

Just the fact that you picked up this book means that you are already seeking wisdom and understanding. You are hungry to understand more about your human experience, higher consciousness and communicating with yourself on a soul level. Even if this book was filled with nothing but vegan recipes and photos of my cat, just acknowledging that you were curious enough to learn more about your gifts of being an empath shows that you've begun the transformation of awareness already! Go you!!

Lastly, this book is a partnership between you and Spirit. Set the intention now of how you would like to benefit from reading this book.

What would be your Highest outcome from reading this book?

_____

_____

_____

_____

_____

_____

_____

_____

THE EMPATH QUIZ

Are You an Empath?

1. Do you tend to feel exhausted being around a lot of other people? Overwhelmed by large crowds?	Yes	No
2. Do you need alone time in order to recharge? Do you sometimes need an entire day to feel ready to be around others again?	Yes	No
3. Have you been told that you are too sensitive or too emotional?	Yes	No
4. Do you have a negative reaction to graphic images or violence on television and movies; for example, people hurting other people or animals?	Yes	No
5. Do you have trouble sleeping? Do you struggle with bouts of insomnia?	Yes	No
6. Can you feel other people's emotions, stress and pain? Do you find yourself absorbing their energetic mood swings?	Yes	No
7. Are you interested in alternative healing topics and practices such as meditation, energy work, reiki, tarot or anything else metaphysical?	Yes	No
8. Do you suffer from frequent or unexplained anxiety and/or depression? Do you sometimes feel nervous for no reason?	Yes	No

9. Are you uncomfortable with confrontation and arguments to the point where you sometimes feel physically sick from it?	Yes	No
10. Do you get overstimulated in environments with too much demanding your attention; for example, a lot of people talking to you at once, bright lights and loud noises, etc.?	Yes	No
11. Are you aware of any intuitive gifts, such as clairvoyance, clairsentience, claircognizance and clairaudience?	Yes	No
12. Do you absorb and take on other people's emotions and stress when you are near them or interacting with them?	Yes	No
13. Do you ever just "know" when someone needs something, or understand the thoughts of others?	Yes	No
14. Have you had recurring issues with self-esteem and lacking self-love throughout your life?	Yes	No
15. Do you have a pattern of attracting narcissistic people and allowing them to drain your energy?	Yes	No
16. Have you struggled with addictive behaviors in your life?	Yes	No
17. Do you keep your feelings to yourself for fear that it might upset someone else, even if what you sense is true?	Yes	No
18. Do you feel completely recharged and invigorated when spending quality time out in nature?	Yes	No
19. Are food and your emotions tightly linked in your life?	Yes	No
20. Are you the "mother or father" of your group? Do you always make sure everyone is taken care of, even if it's at the expense of your own well-being?	Yes	No

21. Do you find people who need emotional support are often attracted to you and will tell you their whole life story? Are you the person everyone comes to for advice, support and healing?	Yes	No
22. Do you have major anxiety when you feel bound, like you're being controlled or feeling imprisoned?	Yes	No
23. Do you have difficulty spending time in environments with harsh lighting and loud or unexpected noises?	Yes	No
24. Do you often feel totally misunderstood when it comes to your feelings and intentions?	Yes	No
25. Are you often more comfortable being around animals or babies than other people?	Yes	No

If you answered yes to the majority of these questions, chances are you are an empath. You are a natural "feeler" and in tune with the energy of your environment, as well as those you are connecting to.

If you identify as an empath, yet you have not learned what that means for your life or how to manage your own energy, keep on reading! Being as sensitive as you are takes a whole lot of strength to be in this world. It comes with its own set of responsibilities and ways to care for self. So keep going, there is much to cover and much to do!

PART II

THE
PROGRAM

W E E K 1

IDENTIFY --
WHAT IS AN EMPATH?

In the mainstream understanding, an empath is portrayed much like a unicorn or a dragon in the sense that it is often considered something out of a fantasy novel or science fiction movie. It is difficult for mainstream to believe that a person can have innate extrasensory abilities that allows them to *know* things without logical reasoning. When a child knows what the parent is thinking or a person can communicate with an animal, it's just too mystical of a phenomenon for many to accept easily.

Usually cognitive dissonance kicks in.

The parent will ask the child "How did you know that? Did you overhear me saying something earlier?"

Or an audience may dismiss an animal communicator as just being familiar with animals and reading obvious signals.

There's often a lot more that goes into the magic of empathy, and being an empath is much more common than one might think!

An empath can also be considered a "clear feeler." Someone who has the ability to sense beyond what meets the eye. Bypassing appearance, empaths use other tools and finely tuned senses to cut through false information and illusion. They are able to consider a whole array of other areas of information when interpreting a situation, environment or person.

To put it quite simply, an empath is a very wise human being and one of the furthest things from fantasy. Empaths are the some of most real, down-to-earth beings to exist!

Let's take this concept of empath and break it down a bit further.

At the most basic level, all human beings come pre-wired to receive energetic information. This comes built-in to the human experience. In order to perceive the world around you, you must be able to receive information one way or another in order to take in the data input from your environment.

For example, when you put your hand near a pot boiling on the stove, your body will read the energetic information input of the heat. Your nerves will send the signal to your brain, which will then register this information as a different experience than when the pot wasn't boiling. Ideally, if everything is working as it should, your brain will alert the body that the heat is dangerous and to respond appropriately by pulling your hand away from the threat of injury.

This process as you know it obviously happens very rapidly since you are usually quick to pull your hands away from high sources of heat. However, when you break this process down, there is a lot of communication and signaling that is happening within your "wiring" that allows this process to successfully protect you.

It begins as the body initially registers the heat. It isn't until further into this sensory process that you decide that heat from a stove equals danger. You also have to evolve initially to make the discernment ultimately, meaning chances are you learn what hot means by getting burned by things that are hot.

In this example, at the most basic level, you can see how the majority of humans are wired to receive the information of heat. It is up to our life experience and understanding through learning that you are able to interpret your senses that say "hand on heat = bad." This allows you to respond appropriately and protect yourself by pulling your hand away. The same can be true for receiving empathic information because it is all energetic input.

So, no matter what your path is in life or what perceived limitations you may be working through, if you are living in a human body having a human existence, on a base level, you are able to receive and experience energy. And you do!!

Humans are all wired to receive energetic information. We've got the tools built right into our miraculous meat suits! It is important to learn how to use the tools you were given and find out what areas you can develop.

The questions that remain are *to what degree* and *what specialty*?

Step 1: Varying Degrees of Empathy

Your level of consciousness (or self-awareness) and your skills of empathy go hand in hand. Depending on your soul origin, your operational skills of tuning into the human body to receive and accurately interpret the energetic information will vary. It all depends on the wisdom that you bring in through your awareness and embody. This is done by connecting with your Higher self, your multidimensional presence.

For example, a very young soul that has not lived many lifetimes or has not gone through many trainings does not come bearing the same depth of inner wisdom as an older soul. Therefore the young soul may experience a lack of common sense when it comes to their own self awareness or misinterpret subtle communications within their own being.

When the human body which is already designed with natural sensors to receive energetic information through heightened senses, if there is nothing in place to interpret what the energy is communicating, important information will be missed.

Conversely, the opposite is also true. Those who come to Earth bearing the soul gifts of healer, nurturer, guide, teacher, counselor, coach, psychic, and the like, have lived many, many lifetimes. When you live many, many lifetimes and have many past iterations of soul self, you integrate many, many lessons.

These lessons can be experienced in varying degrees from suffering trauma to experiencing bliss and everything in between. This is all experienced in order to achieve a deeper understanding of the energy in the soul's eternal quest for knowledge and thus bring with it... you guessed it, wisdom!

In an empath, the body is picking up the energetic information by natural design, then the imprinted soul's wisdom is applied through the use of self awareness. With continued practice and familiarity of one's own process, an empath can get pretty fluid in understanding the different energies being processed.

As an example, someone who is less aware of their own energetic processing system may get the chills for seemingly no rational reason. They may search for a cool breeze or cold draft to explain what has caused these chills. Or worse, fear may kick in and the mind may create a story that triggers disempowerment, like they suspect a ghost is nearby.

In an empath, it is the wisdom of the empath's higher self that takes this information and communicates from a higher understanding. The body says simply "I have chills." The Higher self may add to that "Pay attention to something right now. Alert!"

Taking that even further would be to consider a fully managed empath who has mastered their skills. They may be able to interpret the chills as a message to say "Pay attention! Positive energy flowing! This is truth that you are discussing right now and your Higher self is supporting it!"

Simply put, our bodies pick up the energy. Higher wisdom interprets it. The free will implements it.

Since we are always receiving energetic information into our systems, the true magic occurs when we learn how to interact with it and communicate with it.

When input is received, the empath has an opportunity to respond, matching the energy received, by giving the subject their complete focus, much like a conversation! We will go more into this later (see Week 9, Interplay: Develop a Language).

Communication is a fundamental aspect for any successful empath. As a matter of fact, many empaths will exhibit an interest in different languages or alternative ways of communication at some point in their life. Whether an empath is communicating with their parent, an animal, or even their own body, much more clarity is produced when the energy exchange is treated like a conversation.

Step 2: Being an Empath is Not a Curse, You're a Gift to Humanity!

To say that empaths are frequently misunderstood is an understatement. Empaths are often labeled as overly sensitive, high maintenance, moody and emotional, bleeding hearts or too naive for your own good.

One thing I've learned over the course of my life is that it takes a lot of strength to be sensitive!

To be constantly bombarded with the energetic "noise" on a planet that has had very little energetic awareness is a life lesson of survival in itself. Fortunately, the collective awareness is evolving, undergoing a massive shift in consciousness, and people are getting wise to the existence of alternative realities. We are even learning how energy plays a major roll in the creation of our current reality. But it's a slow process.

When you are an empath, you come by these sensitivities naturally. Many empaths are born with their senses wide open! I call this being "born with your lights on."

Empaths have the ability to connect with the energetic consciousness of another being. Ideally, this ability can be used as the divine gift that it is when the empath is able to gauge the sensory input to understand and translate or transmit the information. When unaware of what is happening, however, you are prone to absorb a lot of energetic static that isn't yours, resulting in what I call "frequency entanglement." Over time this can result in empathic stress or empathic overload.

If you were born into a family that had no idea how to manage their own energy or listen to the song of their own souls, chances are you are quite familiar with empathic overload. More often than not, children will develop coping mechanisms in order to learn how to navigate life in their own unique way because no one in their life is sensitive to their energy, not to mention teaching them how to manage it.

Maybe you were one of these children. Maybe you never really understood yourself or what makes you so unique until you went on your own inner quest later in life. Maybe you are just now beginning to uncover just how very precious you are! In any case, you know exactly what I mean when I say it takes a lot of strength to be sensitive.

Many empaths experience different approaches to the same soul lesson over and over again through out their lifetime. Ultimately, this is a major benefit because you are simply gaining more information ammo for your intuitive arsenal = wisdom. However, the empathic path is not always an easy one, especially if you have to go through difficult or even painful life lessons to learn more about yourself, which is often the case.

The repetition of emotional pain patterns and karmic cycles in an empath's life serve as strengthening experiences. I'm not saying it is always fair or pleasant or even comfortable, because usually it is not. But much like forged steel that has been hardened by fire, over the life time, the empath learns how to protect themselves, clear and transmute their energy and ultimately empower themselves allowing more movement and freedom in their life.

This is my wish for every empath out there; healing, empowerment and freedom!

Empaths are not just fragile overly-emotional creatures that exist to get overwhelmed by what they're feeling and hide away from the world (although in some cases that really is the best course of action).

No, empaths are here to activate their feeling panels like it's a dusty gauge on the ol' existential dashboard. We got 'em! Why not use 'em!

Feelings and sensations are incredibly important ways to navigate both our inner and outer worlds, yet our emotions and ability to tune into ourselves have long been suppressed.

Not that this is a fair deal at all, but there is a reason that emotions and clarity of mind have been hijacked for centuries by controlling powers. It is because when you are empowered, you are powerful! Imagine a world where empowered empaths were the norm. This world would be a kinder, healthier, happier and more abundant place to live!

Unfortunately, the hijacking of human power is real. This has been a deep wound that humanity has carried and has caused a great imbalance of energy on this planet. Again, due to the massive shift in consciousness that the world is currently going through, the dense stronghold has been losing its grasp of control. Empaths are waking up, more and more by the day, and you are a part of it!

By simply realizing there might be something more to this physical experience you are having on planet Earth is a marker of grand progress. You don't need to have all the answers just yet. Quietly begin by listening to your curiosity, your inner knowing, that there is something more to your feelings to explore — because there is!

Step 3: Path of Love vs. Path of Fear

As an empath, your feelings and sensitivities are the key to your gifts. No two empaths are identical in the way you experience energy, or even interpret it. There are many spectrums of the senses in which you can "read" energy, which is why one empath might be more "sensitive" to a certain stimulation than another.

Once you start paying attention to your feelings, sensations, emotions and overall state of being, the better you can monitor them to know thyself. You do this by not attaching to any of the feelings or creating a story around it. Instead, by remaining in the state of observation, you can learn from them. They are energetically communicating with you. Think of being a good listener in a conversation, only you are having a conversation with your feelings and giving them a chance to share what they need to communicate.

The only reason why you would hold onto an emotion longer than to watch it pass by is if your soul is telling you that there is something more to explore here. There may be some healing to be done here. We can often have emotion attached to a past traumatic experience, painful story or limiting belief that we have been taught. When these emotions are triggered, it is always, always, always an indiction that deeper work needs to be done so that you may return to the state of observation and not attachment. Without doing this healing work, we become prisoners to the pain patterns which ultimately lowers our vibration and auric resonance.

Allowing these emotions to move and flow through you allows you to assess them as a whole. This equates to a whole other level of conscious than simply reactionary.

e-motion = energy in motion

For example, if I'm feeling upset that a friend didn't call by the time she said she would, I could attach to the emotion and react based on that emotion. I could stay angry and stew in it so when I did talk to her eventually, I'd be uptight, bitter and expect an apology for her being so inconsiderate. Alternatively, if I allow myself to feel the feeling without attachment and observe, I would see how this is highly unusual and unexpected for her to forget our appointment and maybe my intuition is indicating concern for her well being. I could then respond with love, instead of reacting out of anger, by calling her to find out that she is all right.

Each emotion is a data point to consider as a part of a greater whole. So go with the flow and see where your soul guides you. The more you explore, the more you will find. You are a multifaceted, multidimensional being. There is much to see!

Your emotions serve as an indicator for your overall vibration and is the easiest way to tell you when your energy is clear or if you may be off or influenced by a lower vibrational energy force.

Our life force energy is a powerful force that flows through our entire being made up of multiple bodies of consciousness, but it can be interfered with if we are carrying energy that is not ours or no longer serves us. The most powerful thing we have on this planet is the love that is created and shared by the lights of our hearts and we are most powerful when our hearts are clear!

We may be a complicated network of energy systems but it doesn't have to be so complicated to understand how to read our own energy.

There is a sure-fire way to know what vibration you are holding in your energy field every single time. Take a look at your emotions — are you operating from the path of love? Or the path of fear?

Path of Fear = Low Vibration

fearful	envious	worried
angry	bitter	shameful
jealous	resentful	entitled
guilty	spiteful	victimized
anxious	self pity	lacking

Zero Point = Neutral

open	unattached	single point focus
flow state	balanced	stable

Path of Love = High Vibration

curiosity	gratitude	compassion
excitement	contentment	forgiving
joy	peace	nurturing
pleasure	bliss	generosity
creativity	empathy	laughter

Knowing that you are an empath and are tuned into feeling things clearly, you will have a leg up when armed with this information. The formula is simple: if you are in a low vibration emotion and you take action, such as make a decision or react, then you will receive more of that low vibration energy. The converse is true. If you are in a high vibration emotion and you take action, such as make a decision or share your light with those around you, you will receive the same energy back from the universe.

This is universal law of consciousness as it follows quantum physics.

Sounds high tech but it really is very simple. Not always easy, but simple. It takes conscious focus and consistent intention.

If you find you are feeling low, hanging out and kicking rocks down the path of fear, make a conscious decision to shift your energy before taking any action. Don't call your mother because you feel guilty. That conversation won't go well. Don't keep that job because you're afraid you won't find a better one. It'll just become harder to maintain.

As an example, I tend to make poor food choices when I'm feeling sad or anxious. But when I'm feeling the love and my energy is clear, I will always, always reach for those fruits and veggies. Those are much higher vibrational foods that do a body good.

The quickest way to shift low vibrational energy is to shift right on into gratitude. It doesn't matter how simple it is, if you focus on something you are grateful for, you can build upon it. If you ate today and were able to breathe clean air, you've already got two things you can add to your list. Try it!

Let's make a list of 8 things you are grateful for:

1._____   4._____   7._____
2._____   5._____   8._____
3._____   6._____

Play with this formula in your own life whenever you're feeling the funk. Watch what happens as a result. If you're feeling low, it's a no go. If you've got that high vibe, the possibilities are open wide.

And if the higher vibrational energy doesn't come back to you immediately, just give it a moment. It always eventually comes around.

Step 4: 30 Signs You're an Empath

Do you suspect that you may be one of these fantastic spiritual creatures? How much of the list below do you relate to?

1. **Anxiety** — we all have anxiety. It is a part of being human, sadly, a part of daily life. The anxiety that correlates to being an empath would be a long-term chronic condition that has been affecting you for much of your life despite efforts and various treatment. Such as the inability to cope with your own anxiety, easily being inundated with feelings of overwhelm. A constant sensation of your fight-or-flight response being triggered.

2. **Inner knowing, clear knowing** — without being told specific information or overhearing conversations, you already have the information. Things tend to not come as a surprise once revealed.

3. **Being overwhelmed in public spaces** — Shopping malls, stadiums, restaurants, schools, stage-fright in classroom or any time of being in front of or around a lot of other people and a lot of other people's energies. Group settings, live chats, live streams, phone calls and having to "be on" can also cause this sense of overwhelm.

4. **Feeling other people's emotions as if they're your own** — this can be tricky especially when you don't realize

what is actually going on. You can absorb other people's emotions when you are around them and own them as if they're your own, not even realizing that they aren't even organic to your own energy. You can walk into a place and feel suddenly irritable. Even if you've had a great morning, a delicious breakfast, no traffic on the way, but once you get there, anger sets in. It can be confusing to pinpoint where this is coming from when you feel it so clearly, when really it could be the mood that your coworker is in and may or may not be expressing openly.

5. **Watching violence on tv, movies, news, stories is a no-go** — these tend to make you uncomfortable, skeeze you out, makes your body tense up, gives you nightmares, changes your mood and vibration, or can replay in your mind when you don't want to be reminded of it.

6. **Having an inner lie detector** — you may find that you just know when someone is lying or not. It's like an inner compass that registers when something is "true north." This can come in handy when harnessed and utilized like as a lawyer or a parent. But when an unmanaged empath, you can run the risk of knowing when someone is lying to you, but giving them a pass without accountability. You may even internalize why they lied as a reflection of your own value.

7. **Absorbing physical symptoms of another** — a lot of medical empaths have this ability. Let's say you are visiting a family member that is sick and they are experiencing stomach issues. Your stomach may give you pain and discomfort. When you go to use the bathroom or even leave, you may find the symptoms alleviate on their own

only to return when you return to the company of your sick family member. Before assuming a random ailment is yours, always test your own physical symptoms by removing yourself from the energy in your environment to see if the symptoms will dissipate on their own.

8. **Digestive disorders and lower back problems** — this shows how we may absorb energy that doesn't belong to us. Since we don't know how to clear it, process it, or release it, it can become stuck within our own energy system, typically within the lower chakras. This can flare up when under stress or duress. For example, interacting with your domineering boss may cause your back pain to flare up. More on chakras later (Week 4, Ignite — Chakras and Raising Vibration).

9. **Always rooting for the underdog** — in movies, stories or even real life situations, you are identifying with or cheering on the person who does not have the obvious advantage. Feeling bad for the guy who gets kicked around, beat up and the nice guys who really do finish last. Maybe even talking to people just to be nice, or doing things out of pity.

10. **People tell you their whole life story within minutes of meeting them** — including people offloading all of their life problems onto you. Some may reveal parts of themselves that they don't openly share with others, like their deepest, darkest secrets. "Oh my gosh, I haven't told that to anyone" may be a phrase you hear often. People can feel your energy as a safe haven, so they freely want to spill all and tell you everything. They may even want to use you as a sounding board to bounce ideas off of in

areas where they may be judging themself. Empaths tend to be incredibly nonjudgemental and understanding when it comes to others, and incredibly critical when it comes to your own perspective on yourself.

11. **Constant fatigue** — constantly being bombarded by other people's energy, whether they're sharing their life with you, you're picking up on their emotions or physical ailments, it's draining! It's exhausting. It's really easy to find yourself feeling really tired no matter how much sleep you're getting or what kind of diet you have. You can be doing something you really love or pampering yourself to the fullest extent, and still feel completely exhausted. This also plays a role in those who suffer from "mystery illnesses" like chronic Lyme disease and Fibromyalgia. If you are in an unbalanced relationship dynamic, over time a person can literally drain you of your life force energy, leaving you depleted. More on energy vampires later (Week 2, Illuminate — The Unmanaged Empath).

12. **Addictions** — exploring addictive nature within personality, drugs, social media, sugar, sex, gambling, working, shopping, gaming, attention, food, etc. It is even possible to be addicted to fear in which you remain in a state of anxiety triggered by external stimulants that you choose to surround yourself with. You may currently be in active addiction right now or historically have moved through phases of battling addiction. This is quite common among empaths and sensitive souls, especially during the times of youth. This is because you know on some level there is something better to be experienced other than the world you are currently experiencing. There is something more towards ultimate satisfaction and satiation that is embedded within your soul,

but while in this Earthly plane, it is difficult to find that kind of peace. You may try different means of finding something close to it, like through food, drugs, work, making money, spending money, etc. Someone who is really sensitive, it can be all too easy to get caught in that cycle of addiction because you just get so set on trying to fill that need to experience peace and ultimately relief. Of course certain substances have addictive qualities by nature, but there is more to it when energetically predisposed.

13. **Naturally drawn to healing** — Whether it be exploring different methods and modalities of healing, talking to galactic beings, connecting to angels, playing with fairies, practicing Reiki, natural religions, psychics, herbalism, energy work, somatic therapy, whatever falls under the umbrella. That's your inner self guiding you to find out more because this applies to you. This seeking will help you find the answers, healing and expansion on your own journey. Follow your heart!

14. **Being innately creative** — if you were a very creative child, drawn towards painting, singing, dancing, crafting, comedy, sculpting, building, imagining, or other ways of tapping into your creative energy. Your creativity may lie in other areas as well, such as taking apart old electronics to build something new out of the old parts, or finding a way to make your bike go faster than all the other kids' bikes in the neighborhood. Even coming up with creative lies to talk your way out of getting in trouble uses your imagination! Creativity knows no bounds. You may be creative in problem-solving, business, negotiating terms within relationships. Creativity, where there wasn't something, and now there is something. You are the catalyst. You are the creator.

15. **Love of nature and animals** — need I say more? Every meme ever made about being that person who makes friends with the dog at the party instead of making friends with the people, yeah, that is talking about empaths.

16. **Need for solitude** — knowing yourself well enough that when you are feeling out of whack, it's time to take some downtime. Whether it be taking a mental health day from work or scheduling an entire day where you don't need to cook, clean or even change out of your pajamas. Sometimes resting and recuperation is just what the doctor ordered! Sure, you can go, go, go and keep up with the rat race of life. There's always something that needs to be done. But if you don't honor your natural rhythm of taking a break to recharge every once in a while, you may get a lot of colds or get sick easily. This is your body's way of making you rest when you're not taking the initiative. Great books and a cup of tea, spending time in the gazebo in the yard, going away for the weekend, or just getting a mani-pedi at the spa. Whatever it is, you need that alone time to recalibrate. Essentially what you're doing is shifting the focus away from the energy of others so that you can check in and assess what's going on with your own energy. This is an integral part of maintenance as an empath. If you don't take the time to recharge, you will find that your patience will become shorter. You will feel mentally foggy. You will make more mistakes. You might even be clumsier. You're just not showing up 100% and you know it.

17. **Gets bored or distracted easily** — not all empaths can relate to this as a general truth, but if something doesn't really speak to you or resonate with you, good luck making

you pay attention! I remember during my school years, the administration was pretty eager to test and diagnose us "sensitive kids" with ADD and ADHD. This sent a very damaging message that we, as kids, were broken somehow and not the "norm." How surprised they were to find out that my IQ was higher than most and I was simply bored and not invested in the curriculum. Empaths process information much differently, and so learning styles, attention and focus will differ from the "norm."

18. **It's impossible to do things that you don't enjoy doing —** The more you move forward on your spiritual journey and declutter your life of commitments, people, obligations and patterns that no longer resonate with you, you will find this becomes even more laborious to do things you don't want to do. It's almost unbearable. Where maybe you used to sit through a class that you didn't enjoy, or sit through church or some kind of family obligation, like the neighbor that you met once having a baby shower, and just grin and bear it the whole time. Now you just can't do it. Even small talk may be unbearable where you struggle to find the polite, surface conversation because you may find it easier to talk about what is really going on in the world. Anything fake, surface or vapid is just not fun and thus insufferable.

19. **Strives for truth —** This can tie in with your inner lie-detector. Having a conversation with someone that you just know is trying to pull the wool over your eyes. As an example, if you encounter a salesman who obviously has an agenda. You're in conversation and you can just feel that everything that is coming out of their mouth is just blatantly not correct or not resonating with you. You may be quick

to move on to the next thing once you have deemed this person an untrustworthy source of information. You may also be constantly googling things and researching things in order to get to the bottom of what is the truth. You may feel this way when it comes to purchases, new job possibilities, relationships or even the state of the world. Just a constant desire to have the truth. You want to know. You must know!

20. **Always looking for more answers and knowledge** — You feel a deep truth that the more information you have, the more powerful you are. The better decisions you can make. The smarter play you can make on the game board of life. All the information available, even if it is an ugly truth, you'd prefer to have the truth to know what you're working with.

21. **You might like adventure and freedom** — this doesn't necessarily mean eating exotic cuisine like deep fried crickets and vacationing at nude beaches unless that's your thing, but anything that promotes feelings of liberation and freedom is a tell-tale empath trait. For example, the idea of becoming debt-free or mortgage free, travel as a part of your career, living as a minimalist in a tiny house, starting your own business and being self-employed are all ways to express this desire for adventure and freedom.

22. **Detests clutter** — you may feel most comfortable and do your best work in a tidy and clear space. It doesn't even have to be a large space. Having an organized environment promotes feeling organized and focused on the inside allowing your energy and focus to flow easier. As an unmanaged empath, you may actually be living in a cluttered situation and feel weighed down by the clutter of your life. Clutter comes in all forms. Clutter of

commitments, clutter of stuff, clutter of relationships and desire to free yourself but feel overwhelmed as to where to begin.

23. **Love to daydream and doodle** — constantly daydreaming and doodling, part of creation, coming up with new ideas and solutions, also creates space to listen to guidance and receive energetic information, transcendental meditation. Daydreaming and doodling are signs of a healthy brain that is using multiple areas simultaneously. For example, you can be in a conversation with a person fully present and attentive while still doodling as you listen to what they are relaying to you. This may actually help you process the information better. Raise your hand if you doodled in class!

24. **Routine, rules and control are too limiting and confining** — feel imprisoned by structure and regiment, military discipline would be polar opposite and create major anxiety. For example, someone who is highly sensitive and empathic who had a career in the military with their life so structured, when they leave the military, they may find difficulty finding balance and may fall into addictive cycles. It is important to grant yourself the space and grace to find your own natural flow after being in such a restrictive structure for so long.

25. **Prone to carry physical weight** — even with a healthy diet and active lifestyle, you find that you always carry weight that is difficult to target and remove. This is not necessarily a medical issue but rather a phenomenon. The weight is present to counterbalance any flighty energy and enhance a grounding effect. It can also act as an energetic barrier, when you are in an environment that would be experienced too harshly otherwise. The weight can be a protective barrier

to absorb some of the dissonance. Also, if you carry energy that is not yours, this can present as weight as well. It is literally impossible to live in this world as it is now and not absorb energetic density. If you are a particularly sensitive empath, weight might be an ongoing, or even lifelong issue, despite your greatest efforts. However, there are things you can do to maintain peak health as a sensitive empath. For example, releasing cords of attachment or removing a negative influence from your life, like a breakup from a toxic relationship, may cause a drop in physical weight as you move forward.

26. **Always told you're an excellent listener** — this goes hand in hand with people feeling comfortable to open up to you. You may be great in business where you hear the genuine needs of the client and respond appropriately. Your friends may come to you often and share the latest juice in their lives or look to you for advice. When first inserted into social situations, you may feel naturally guided to hang back and listen first before asserting yourself.

27. **Absolute intolerance to narcissism** — Anytime you encounter someone who is all about themselves, talking about themselves, focused only on themselves, and they treat those around them like they are all here to just do their bidding, you may find this turns your stomach a bit. You may have even had a relationship in your life whether it be romantic, parental or otherwise, where a narcissistic individual was really close to you during developmental times. You have learned from your experience in this relationship, past, present or otherwise, that you just have no patience for someone with this kind of ego structure because you have learned how draining and soul-sucking it really is.

28. **You can "feel" the days of the week** — you may feel the energy of a Monday compared to the energy of a Friday. You may feel tuned in to the vibe of what each day offers. Whether or not you have the typical Monday through Friday 9-5 kind of job, you may still "feel" into the energy of the day. You could have off on Monday but still experience anxiety on Sunday night and have to remind yourself that you have off in order to subdue your energetic response.

29. **You're not a fan of thrift stores or antiquing** — some empaths (not all) simply prefer not to buy anything that is used. You don't like someone else's used stuff with the smells and the vibes because energy is absorbed from the previous owner or user. Antiques, hand-me-downs and pass-ons are usually a hard no. It is not that you're ungrateful or don't see the value in the item. But naturally, you may feel an aversion to accepting someone else's used, old stuff, especially if there's some funky energy behind it. On the other hand, some empaths really shine at seeing the potential in something old and making it new again. Nothing a little soap and holy water can't fix! That's the creativity kicking in. It just depends on the empath.

30. **You may come off as moody or aloof** — There's a difference between being shy and being totally unapproachable. To someone who doesn't know you well or doesn't know how to "read" you, they might notice the different moods or energies that you are cycling through. Your emotions can be all over the map depending on what you are picking up, what you are absorbing, and what you've

been holding on to, piled on top of what you are naturally feeling in that moment. This smorgasbord of "feels" can create quite the moody confusion within an empath leaving an onlooker to think you're distant.

W E E K   2

ILLUMINATE –
THE UNMANAGED EMPATH

In the quest of empowerment as an empath, it's essential to shine the light on areas that have been hidden from your consciousness. There are many mechanisms in place in this world that prevent you from illuminating the truth behind these things. Good thing empaths can cut through illusion! It just takes a little bit of education, practice and patience with yourself.

The beauty of being an empath is that you are designed to pick up the most subtlest of signals. In a world of density and duality, it can feel a bit harsh to someone whose settings are set to hyper-sensitive. Focusing on the difficulties the world presents for empaths gives a feeling that it would be easier to just cope and manage through life, hiding in the shadows, just to fly below the radar. Instead, my aim is to encourage you and teach you how to understand and embrace your gifts so that you may stand in your power. Imagine if every single person were to do that. Together we can and will change the world.

To be highly sensitive in a lower vibrational world comes with many challenges. One of the main misconceptions that is woven into the fabric of many societies is how sensitivity has long been considered a weakness when it is truly a gift.

You may be familiar with the famous quote about judging a fish by its ability to climb a tree. This could not be more true for many sensitive empaths who attempt to find their belief systems, identities, careers and opinions of themselves often skewed by a lens of misunderstanding due to the lack of support and proper education about energy management.

The danger lies when an empath is anchored in the 3D world and focuses on the external value system while remaining completely unaware of your own gifts and value. In many cases, it can feel like the world is against you, unbearable, and may be too difficult to deal with.

This can lead to victim mentality and getting stuck in the trapping system of illusion which then leads to suffering, illness, trauma or even tragedy.

This may sound dramatic but when an empath who is designed as being so energetically receptive absorbs and becomes majorly influenced by lower vibrational energy, it truly has grave consequences if ignored.

This is why energetic management is an essential part of self care as an empath. You do this by remaining connected to your personal truth and your soul's energetic signature (I will teach you how to do this in Week 3: Influence). To know who you are is to know that all is well. But when absorbing the distorted energies of the outside world, other people, EMFs (electromagnetic frequencies), and other lower frequencies, it is like static in the airwaves of an empath. Your own energy becomes extremely unclear.

When we receive all of this energetic information but don't have the ability to translate, transmit or transmute it, it becomes a burden.

We need to develop our sensory systems and keep energy clear through our awareness and consistent intention.

Remember the example covered in Week 1 about getting the chills:

Unmanaged Empath — the body says it has the chills and the unmanaged empath wonders what is wrong, tries to get warm or is fearful they're getting sick because that guy at work was coughing a lot and there's this thing going around and maybe I wasn't as cautious as I should've been and maybe I need to take some medicine for it or go get tested and see a doctor to tell me what's wrong with me... and so it goes.

Empowered Empath — the body gets the chills, the empath knows this is a communication so they pay closer attention or become more alert, staying open and paying attention to the rest of their sensory system in order to feel further into it and gain a deeper understanding of what the communication may be.

Master Empath — the body get chills, the master empath registers this indicator without emotional attachment, while simultaneously registering a tickle in their lower abdomen and an itch in the left eye while looking at a orange cat crossing the street and listening to a song on the radio about true love, all indicating a very clear message that the empath is able to decipher with precision based on the intuitive language the master empath has developed for themself.

A balanced and masterful empath is much like an eagle in nature. The eagle has the ability to hone its focus so precisely that it can spot a mouse in a field from 2 miles away in the air. It can also soar at the highest altitude of all the birds while taking in a large land area, surveying the best course of action to take next, all without feeling overwhelmed. The eagle has the ability to dial its focus into a laser beam or take in the big picture without getting inundated or stressed out by all the information it is assessing.

Mastering your skills of empathy is completely possible. It is all about finding your energetic balance and maintaining it. When you are first starting out, this is much easier said than done. Often times, it is easier to start getting clear on what may be out of balance for your energetic state to remain balance and remove what is not serving you from your energy field.

Step 1: Frequency Entanglement

When your energy is tainted and tangled with frequencies that do not serve you or resonate with you, it throws the entire system out of alignment. Then, from this imbalanced place, you manifest undesirable results like toxic relationships, unfortunate events and situations that don't accurately reflect who you are or what you want. This is all occurring because you're not operating from your own pure energetic signature.

In order to better understand how frequency entanglement affects you, imagine this: it's a beautiful summer afternoon. You are driving down the road with the windows down to enjoy the fresh air and you've got some really great music playing. You're really enjoying the whole vibe that you've got going on in your own vehicle.

Then you pull up to a stop light. There is a car next to you on your left. They also have their windows down. They are also blasting their music, which is a totally different vibe than yours. Then to your right, a motorcycle pulls up with his music blaring and glass pack exhaust throttling. Not only would it be pretty hard to hear your music clearly anymore, but the whole vibe you had going on just became totally interrupted by what other people have going on. That's frequency entanglement.

This is why it is crucial to clear and untangle your energy from anything that isn't yours as a regular practice.

If you are just starting out on the journey of understanding yourself and your energy, you may feel like cleaning your spiritual house is equivalent to tidying up a hoarder's house. It may feel daunting to start. It does get easier in time as this will become a lifestyle practice rather than an overnight fix.

Step 2: Health Issues

The body being the loudest messenger, the unmanaged empath tends to ignore the messages that your body is sending to you, especially when the messages are disruptive to your life.

Unfortunately, this means that an unmanaged empath is more likely to experience serious or reoccurring health issues if you remain ignorant to your own energetic reality.

Human beings are made up of multiple bodies of consciousness, meaning you have many systems in place that work together and relay energetic information. More on these later. The way these tend to work is in a trickle-down effect. If your higher consciousness is trying to send you a message for your highest good and you aren't paying attention, it will work it's way down each body of consciousness in order to get "louder."

It may look something like this: imagine you are in a toxic relationship that is draining your energy and keeping your vibration low. It may be a relationship that you have outgrown or no longer serves your overall health and happiness. If nothing is evolving there or changing for the better, your intuition may be nudging you subtly that maybe this isn't the best relationship for you. Sadly, it is very easy to ignore your intuition as an unmanaged empath because there are much more things that distract you and clamor for your attention.

The energy may begin to build up in your causal body which will ultimately block energy flow. You may find you have problems with finances or things turning out well due to your blocked energy preventing a free flow of life force energy.

If the message is not received that something is up, you may be struck with a situation or display in front of you to connect with your mental body. You may watch or read something learning how a toxic relationship truly resembles your current situation.

If you choose to deny that this applies to you or make any changes, over time, this energy will trickle down into your emotional body. You may start feeling depression or uninspired with life, feeling low vibrational emotions often. You may deal with daily general anxiety and just feel uptight. Surprisingly, many people can still choose to ignore how they are feeling about things. When there are so many addictive methods and devices available so people can check out of their own unhappiness, it's much easier to continue to ignore the energetic messages. By getting a false boost of dopamine from something external like checking social media or playing a video game, it's easier to trick oneself into the notion that you are fine and coping. By this point, the energetic density has trickled into the physical body.

Once the physical body is housing the truth of you being out of balance with your soul, it will send you the loudest messages. You may have back aches preventing you from moving. You may have migraines causing you to literally stop everything and regenerate your energy.

Whenever there is a health crisis or longterm illness, this is often viewed as a fearful event. We often put our trust into the hands of "professionals" who can tell us what is going on with our body. We have been conditioned to listen to someone else outside of ourselves who "knows better" when the truth of the matter is that you have all of the answers within.

– Personal Share –

My entire spiritual awakening journey began with a chronic mystery illness that left me bedridden and wheelchair bound for over 3 years. I was completely debilitated as I couldn't bathe, clothe or feed myself. I had frequent events of what I called "pain seizures" where every muscle in my body would tighten and spasm to the point of excruciating pain while I was conscious for the whole episode. This would last for sometimes up to 15 minutes at a time. Each doctor I visited would diagnose me with something different and put me on a different medication or expensive therapy. Yet, no one was able to offer me a an explanation of what was going on or a treatment or therapy to resolve my issues. No one had any answers. No one knew of a cure.

I had gotten to a point where I no longer wanted to be alive because I was literally suffering in excruciating pain every moment of the day.

At this point in my journey, I was an unmanaged empath; very unaware of energy and how my alignment affected everything. Yet, I knew I had a decision to make if life were to continue. Since it was clear that I didn't want to give up on life just yet, I prayed for a miracle.

It first came in as a tiny feeling of hope that all was not lost. It was the tiniest notion. I could not explain this feeling at the time but it was the most optimistic sensation I had felt in a long time. Very slowly I started to feel guided to make small changes. Now that my energy was open after praying and hoping for a miracle, my intuition was able to start flowing in, slowly but surely.

It started with little steps like switching from drinking soda to only water and seltzer. I then started to ween myself off all the pharmaceutical medications they were pumping into my system. I swore off eating gluten-filled and processed food and added more vegetables to my diet. I started to listen to guided meditations and even made an appointment with a shaman, which was totally new for me.

Eventually, I started feeling well enough to pull myself out of bed. Then I could take myself to the toilet. Then I could walk a little outside. Then a little more. The momentum started to build on its own. Pretty soon I was able to go up and down stairs again. Then I was driving again. Then I was working again. Then I was able to leave the abusive marriage and toxic family environment I had been living in for so long. Then I was able to go back to school and finish my degree. Then I was able to start my own business. And the story continues on from there.

It took many years for me to clean up and align my life so that it matched my heart and soul. It's been 11 years since I first sat in that wheelchair.

Energy is everything! I can tell you now with a smile on my face, I haven't even had a cold in years.

- - -

If you have health issues, especially if they are serious or ongoing, you can be certain that there is something more going on. Begin your physical healing process by looking into the energetic reasons behind the ailment. There are many modalities that support physical healing through an energetic approach such as somatic body work, meditation, plant medicine, emotion code therapy, medical intuitive or medical medium and many others.

Reading List!

There are a number of excellent books written on decoding physical ailments. Some of my favorites include:

1. *Heal Your Body, by Louis Hay*
2. *Your Body's Telling You Love Yourself, by Lise Bourbeau*

Step 3: Narcissists and Energy Vampires

One of the biggest culprits for an unmanaged empath to lose their peace is to continue attracting narcissists and energy vampires. These culprits just love empathic energy and especially if the empath doesn't have any self awareness or personal boundaries to fend them off.

If an empath is carrying any energetic wounds, such as a difficult childhood or painful breakup, this is a guaranteed "in" for these energy draining egomaniacs. It is very tricky for an unmanaged empath to recognize the potential threat because they are often cloaked in kinships or having something in common, like a common bond. For example, the narcissist often uses the approach of trauma bonding, which is relating to the unmanaged empath wound-to-wound or trauma-to-trauma, rather than heart to heart. It will seem like a heart based connection because unmanaged empaths carry their emotional baggage in their hearts, so they may never suspect this person as being dangerous or unhealthy. The unmanaged empath is quick to understand what they went through or where they are coming from because you can still feel how painfully deep the wounds go within yourself.

The difference between the unmanaged empath and the narcissist is that they are built completely differently, psychologically and energetically. The ego structure of a narcissist is literally build on a foundation of insecurity. This causes a narcissist to live their entire lives and make all their decisions driven solely by the origin of their fears.

A tell-tale sign of a narcissist is someone who uses as little of their own energy (this includes creative energy) as possible and instead redirects your life force energy for their own gain. The Kardashians have literally built a multibillion dollar empire around this basic formula, just ask all the people filing lawsuits against them for the ideas the stole and sold as their own.

Empaths, narcissists and energy vampires most commonly stem from unbalanced beginnings and varying early developmental trauma. The difference is that empaths choose to rise above it and continue to be of service to those around them, stemming from love (or at least an intention of love, although maybe wounded at times). Narcissists are devoid of desire to be of service and reverse the focus onto themselves.

The term energy vampires don't always have to indicate a narcissistic ego structure, however they can be operating in similar ways. Another wounded unmanaged empath can easily be an energy vampire. Anyone who does not have their own boundaries or does not respect your boundaries is an immediate indication that they are an energy vampire.

Empaths also have to consider the multidimensionality of this dynamic. It's not just about the psychology behind people. Dark energies will also work through spiritually weaker people in order to get to you. If someone lives in a lower vibration, they are more vulnerable to being influenced by a darker being. Keeping people around who are not responsible for or aware of themselves in that capacity leaves you open and susceptible to inviting chaotic, destructive and draining energy into your field.

For example, if you need to tell your Aunt Sally 6 times that you need to get off the phone and she just keeps ignoring what you have stated and continues to go on about all the injustices in her own life, that's an energy vampire. If you have a sister who never takes the time out of her day to check in with you and see how you are feeling or if you need anything, but then expects you to drop everything when she is going through a crisis and she tends to have a lot of crises, that is an energy vampire. If you keep an old friend in your life because you've known them since you were kids and you would feel bad moving on yet they are constantly negative and gossip about everyone yet expects compassion from you, this is an energy vampire. Keeping these people in your sphere will drain your energy.

Anyone and any thing that needs to impose upon your energy in order to feed and get what it needs, is an energy vampire.

Your energy can be siphoned in multiple ways that if you weren't cognizant, you'd never know. Your energy can be drained by having your time taken up, money taken, even just your attention and focus. If you need to focus on a project and have set the boundaries to not be interrupted, yet your family continues to interrupt you without regard and expects you to just be ok with it, those are energy vampires.

Narcissists and energy vampires will often enter into (or even design) toxic codependent dynamics with unmanaged empaths in order to keep the supply chain of energy coming. By making the unmanaged empath feel as if they can't live without the person or cannot break away from the relationship, these life sucking individuals maintain control.

This is not always a conscious plan as many unmanaged empaths who are wounded themselves have grown up in codependent households, so this is all they know. They then become energy vampires by disempowering themselves and depending on another person. This codependency is often misunderstood as love and care but rather it is a distorted version of unconditional love. In a healthy and balanced relationship, two people can form more of an interdependent bond where it is made up of two independent people who then strengthen each other by being together. In a toxic codependent relationship, there is often a greater cost to one person to maintain the relationship, whether it be financially, energetically, emotionally or so on.

There is also mass levels of psychosocial conditioning that plays a role in this as well. Just look at what's considered romantic in the mainstream: "You complete me." "I can't live without you." "You have my heart." "I need you." This conditioning makes it very easy for unmanaged empaths to enter into relationships thinking it is a strong bond, when really it is taking a toll on them.

Removing all narcissists from your life (as difficult as it may be because families are often riddled with them) and enforcing strict boundaries with energy vampires is a necessary step when working to regain your own balance, peace and empowerment. I cannot emphasize the importance of this enough! It is fruitless to continue to fulfill yourself, regenerate and recharge your own energy if you choose to keep people in your life that will take from you until you're empty.

Of course narcissists and energy vampires won't like it when you withdraw your energy from them. They may fight back, guilt trip you, say something nasty, be passive aggressive or pout. Let them. You are cutting off their food supply. You are also healing and protecting your own precious energy.

In a one-on-one session with an empath who was getting psychically attacked and drained, I told my client that no matter how low-key she thinks her life is, when it comes to her energy, she is a celebrity. Everyone wants a piece of her bright light! She needs to remain aware of that fact and protect it like she's shielding herself from a paparazzi of vampires, otherwise she will just keep attracting them and allow them to feed off of her energy.

Over time, the more you practice protecting yourself from these energy draining individuals, you will attract less and less into your life. By raising your vibration and strengthening your boundaries, you essentially become unreachable to these energies. We will talk more about how to do this in Week 6: Insulate.

Reading List!

If your interested in going more in depth on this subject to uncover the patterns that are usually present in these dynamics, there are so many great books written on the phenomenon of empaths and narcissists, as well as energy vampires. Some of my favorites include:

1. *Dodging Energy Vampires, by Dr. Christianne Northup*
2. *Empaths and Narcissists: 2 Books in 1, by Judy Dyer*

Step 4: Addiction

Addiction is an unfortunate reality that many unmanaged empaths find themselves struggling with at some point in their life. As sensitive souls born into a world that has so many challenges and restrictions, it is easy for one to find ways to cope, and even escape, the darker parts of reality.

Addictions come in all forms. Whether it is a stubborn cigarette habit, a tendency towards retail therapy when feeling low, an addiction to checking your phone 300 times a day, or a hardcore drug addiction that completely swallows you whole, the mechanics of addiction are the same. Your brain is relying on this chemical release while you are being propped up by a false sense of comfort.

There are many ways to view the phenomenon of addiction, but it all boils down to one thing: the inability to cope with difficult and heavy emotional realities in life.

From an energetic point of view, the addiction stems from lower vibrational energies being absorbed and stuck within the energy system of the unmanaged empath. Using clairvoyance or "second-sight," one can visibly see dark spots and attachments within the aura and chakra system of the unmanaged empath.

These dark spots are blockages that are equivalent to energetic weights from density that ultimately lowers the overall vibration of the empath. When the empath is living in a lower vibration, their life force energy and creational power goes towards feeding dark beings that are attracted to the pure soul's light. These darker beings ultimately attach, feed off of and influence the unmanaged empath.

These darker beings are interested in keeping this empath's vibration so low that they can continue to feed. Of course they don't want to lose their food source. So they influence the empath to feel disempowered, depressed, desperate and to make self-sabotaging decisions, like introducing them to an addiction, which keeps them in a low vibration at all times. This is why you may hear the expressions about addictions like "living with a monkey on their back" or "fighting their own demons." There is truth to these statements.

No pure soul standing in their full power would be susceptible to thoughts or actions of self-harm. Yet when stuck in the trap of addiction, individuals will make decisions that they know are not "healthy' for them. The dependency on the drug of choice holds more power because it offers them some kind of momentary relief from the stronghold of suffering caused by this density.

From a down-to-earth, practical point of view, sensitive souls often have one or many things working against them from the start of life:

- Born into a family that perpetuates emotional repression
- Living in a culture or society that idealizes function over feeling
- Early onset trauma that was never dealt with
- Raised in belief systems that leave one susceptible to darker energies (negative thought patterns, lower vibration)
- Not given the wellness tools or taught how to cope with challenges, emotional hardships and disappointments
- Never truly feeling safe in life or on Earth no matter how loving family has been
- Living in a fear-based, unbalanced mentality and never receiving the necessary support to heal what needs to be healed before moving forward in life
- Being born with extra-sensory perceptions and not being understood by others or taught what they are experiencing

When enough time goes on in an unmanaged empath's life and these issues are not dealt with, the individual may become desensitized. They learn through the pain and struggle of trying to live a normal life that it would be easier to not have to feel so much, and thus any means of suppressing the emotions and escaping the reality becomes welcome. And so an addiction is born.

The goal for the empath is to raise their vibration so high that these lower beings can't even see you. Your energy is literally out of reach to them because you're vibrating so high! The road out of a life of serious addiction is often a long and arduous one that takes time, vulnerability and very honest self-reflection, but it *IS* possible! And you *ARE* worth it!!

Reading List!

If you or a loved one struggles with addiction, there are so many great books to learn more about how to free yourself from the chains of addiction. My top picks include:

1. *The Body Keeps the Score: Brain, Mind, and Body in the Healing of Trauma, Bessel van der Kolk M.D.*
2. *In the Realm of Hungry Ghosts: Close Encounters with Addiction, Gabor Maté*
3. *Breathing Underwater: Spirituality and the Twelve Steps, Richard Rohr*

Step 5: Sexuality + Romanticism

The topic of love can be such a confusing thing to navigate because we humans rarely know what genuine, unconditional love actually feels like. We are raised in a society where agenda is disguised as love. Where there are confusing terms of what loving actions are or distorted ideas of what it means to be loved. We are taught to look outside of ourselves for cues of acceptance, admiration, appreciation and respect.

We spend money, time, energy, and cognitive fuel on chasing after an idealized version of what love looks like due to our inherent desire to be seen and loved as we are. Yet, all too often we contort ourselves in ways that are driven by subconscious motivations in the attempt to achieve this idea of love we are after. We find ourselves feeling confused, devastated or regretful when we realize we are so far from what feels true and good to our souls.

It isn't until you tap into the God source within that we begin to experientially comprehend what unending, relentless love actually means. Before that happens, it is all too easy to fall for the distorted version of what love looks like; conditional. "As long as you are like this, I will love you." "As long as you do this, you will get what you need." An unbalanced exchange of energy that leaves one feeling depleted, wounded and in dire need of recovery. That is conditional love and it is everywhere in human culture.

Conditional love is finite. There is an end. There are terms. It is a mechanism of control and most often an illusion of something much more meaningful than it is. As soon as the dynamic of control is lost, the conditional love stops. This often comes as a shock to those who have been engaging in a toxic relationship with conditional love rather than the unconditional love they expected it to be.

Empaths especially get tangled up in false ideas about love because they feel the energy of others so deeply and can often mistake it for their own, causing them to fall for scenarios that are not healthy or aligned with what the heart is asking for. When you are trained to look to your external environment for validation and love, it can override any soft, subtle voice within directing you back to true unconditional love. That is a love that knows no bounds. An infinite love without circumstance. The pure heart ALWAYS knows the way to find it.

If an empath grows up in an environment of abuse or neglect, which is more common than not, this presents opportunity for more issues around love and connection later in life. For example, a parent's inability to express or meet the emotional needs of the empathic child may cause the empath to develop an obsession with love and romance later in life. Looking for love in all the wrong places. This entanglement may result in the unmanaged empath feeling confused about their own amorous feelings and emotions.

For example, an empath without proper boundaries and clarity about themselves develops energetic cords of attachment with others extremely easily. They engage in relationships with others, parents, friends, romantic partners, sexual partners, bosses, colleagues, etc. and energy cords are formed between the two individuals. These energy cords, often connecting to specific chakras or the aura as a whole, allow energy to exchange between the individuals. This is often to the detriment of the more sensitive soul who is left to deal with the heavy energy.

If an empath is connected to someone who may not have the cleanest energy, like childhood trauma trapped in the sacral chakra causing overactive hyper-sexual energy, the empath will receive this energy. If the empath has their own unhealed trauma, this becomes even more pronounced as it plays out in the relationship. Imagine it to be like someone else's sewage hose is dumping raw sewage into your energy as long as the cord is connected. This means the emotional baggage and energetic wounds that do not belong to the empath will still be absorbed and experienced by the empath as if it's their own. Specifically, the empath may feel the strong overactive hyper-sexual energy of the other person in their own chakra system.

This may cause the empath to believe that they are the one's who feel the intense sexual attraction to the person who is in fact, the one who is initiating sending sexual energy to the empath. The empath may be confused by what they are experiencing and understand this to mean that they love and are turned on by the person when really it is simply frequency entanglement.

You can see how this becomes very confusing for an empath to process their own true feelings.

Now apply this principle to media, entertainment, religion, family dynamics, capitalism, social structures, peer groups, etc. It becomes even more evident, and maybe a bit overwhelming, at how much can be energetically corded into the sexual and emotional centers of a sensitive being.

Unhealthy energies within sexuality and romanticism often manifest in the following ways:

- Codependency
- Infidelity
- Sexual fetishes
- Sexual issues or disfunction
- Fear of love or sex
- Sex and love addiction
- Serial dating
- Polyamory and polygamy

The original desire is a natural, human desire to be loved, cared for, seen and understood exactly as we are. We all have these motivations at our core. It is what makes humans pack animals and drives us to interact with one another, develop relationships, start families, and carry on the human race through procreation. Yet when distortions in your energetic reality cause this natural drive to be manipulated and preyed upon through vehicles such a marketing, pornography, toxic programming, cultural conditioning and negative role models, your pure expression becomes muddled.

Energetically speaking, your life force energy is the same as your creation energy. Your creation energy is often expressed as sexual energy. But when your sexual energy is tainted by pain, fear, trauma, and restriction, your life force/creation energy is being directed towards reproducing pain, fear, trauma and restriction rather than soul truth, growth and evolution.

In the previous section, we talked about addictions. The addiction to love and sex is often an area that is overlooked and normalized by the mainstream because love is such a fundamentally, intricate part of life. It is not only an essential part of spirituality, but an essential part of human survival. Love is what keeps parents feeding and caring for their young. Love is what keeps the hunters and gatherers feeding the rest of the tribe. Love is also what sells products.

So much of our capitalistic culture has profited from pulling on the heart strings and manipulating these core desires that we all have. In addition, traps have been set within our society to keep individuals stuck in their wounds and trauma so they can continue to be preyed upon.

Sexual fetishes is one area that really preys upon a core wound to keep the individual easily controlled. I've always said, tell me your darkest sexual fetishes and I will show you your deepest wound.

When stuck in the trap of addiction (and a sexual fetish often becomes an addiction), the individual is locked into engaging with and reliving the lower vibrational energy that is embedded within their system. When they are so focused on their lower chakras, it is because there is a block, often an energetic backup of karmic energy, trauma that has never been processed or released. This hyper-focus, on a certain sexual fetish is actually a distraction from the core issue of not having an integral need met or most likely being victimized in some way during life. For example, if a young girl was bullied and neglected by her father during childhood, she may develop a preference or fetish for older men based on the core need to receive love, affection and protection from her father.

This also applies to ancestral karma and trauma that has happened in the family lineage or even one's own past lives. For example, an individual may have ancestors who struggled with famine and starvation in their lifetime. This trauma can then be passed on to manifest as sexual arousal while watching someone eat an abundance of food.

This is why it is absolutely essential to never shame, criticize or judge oneself for having sexual issues, preferences, fetishes, trauma or hangups. There is always a deeper reason you are experiencing the feelings that you feel. By regarding oneself with compassion, nonjudgement and unconditional love, one may begin to untangle what feelings are true to the soul and what have been energetic hitchhikers that have been picked up along the way.

You always have the ability to return to your truth and accept only the vibration of unconditional love into your life. It is your life. Your free will. Your body, mind and soul. Cherish yourself as the precious gift you are and accept nothing less.

Reading List!

If you'd like to dive deeper into these themes that we discussed in this section, the following books are great options to explore more:

1. *Codependant No More: How to Stop Controlling Others and Start Caring for Yourself, Melanie Beattie*
2. *The Love Addiction Workbook: Evidence-Based Tools to Support Recovery and Help You Build Healthy Long-Term Relationships*
3. *Women Who Love Too Much: When You Keep Wishing and Hoping He'll Change, Robin Norwood*

Step 6: Dark Night of the Soul

In shamanism and spiritual healing, depression is often a dark visitor that comes to show us something about ourselves. It almost always has a message that we are otherwise unable to receive until we fall deep down to the bottom of the pit of despair.

What message could possibly exist in this dreary and seemingly endless darkness? You are standing on the threshold of a spiritual transformation!

Before we continue, if you feel like you are at the point where you are questioning whether or not to carry on with life and it has escalated to an urgent level, I encourage you to please reach out and ask for help. There is no shame or judgement when one is struggling with finding meaning in life. Most every sensitive soul I have encountered goes through it at some point in their journey. So please know you are never alone and there are plenty of resources and health care professionals that would love to support you through the trickiest parts of your journey.

Having said that, let's explore what is a Dark Night of the Soul? This is a process of spiritual transformation through the means of depression. There are phases that you move through.

When you're in the midst of the Dark Night of the Soul, it can be extremely challenging, confusing, isolating, and you just feel lost.

The whole purpose of going through this process is because you are on the threshold of discovering your true self. It will shake your foundation enough that you stop, assess your whole life as it stands and discern how you can move further towards your truth.

As you move further into your truth, you become more clear on your divine purpose. You are better able to discover your soul gifts; these are the unique skills, natural abilities and inherent wisdom your soul carries. You come into this life with these soul gifts so you may ground the divine light that you are. You are an empath, a light worker, a starseed, an earth angel. You are a spiritual being and you have a mission on this earth. The more light you bring in simply by being who you truly, authentically are, you are impacting the overall vibration of the planet! You're kind of a big deal.

Before going through the Dark Night of the Soul, sensitive souls tend to get caught in the trappings of density and conditional love. They tend to lead a life of selfishness because this is how you are taught to survive. "What can I gain?" "What can I achieve?" "What's in it for me?" Generosity is often motivated by pain, guilt or fear on some level.

Once moving through the intense process of a Dark Night of the Soul, the focus shifts towards calling the light in and expressing it outwardly. Shining the light that you are and radiating for all to see. Allowing the ego to step aside so your true self may shine through brightly. This leads to living a life that was once self-centered and shifting towards how to be of service in the world and an awareness of the collective connection.

Phase 1: Identity Crisis

You're losing your identity and this can feel terrifying. You are groomed to attach to certain labels and ideas of who you are that when you move into this first phase where you begin to question things that have always been accepted or you notice that things, people or places no longer resonate like they once did, you can be left with an aimless feeling of "so now what?"

This is the phase in which you are disassociating from a persona that you have built based on factors that are not in alignment with your soul truth and this can be shocking. You may even shock people around you as you go through this if those people expect you to be the certain way you have always been.

For example, you've been the top producing pharmaceutical rep for a company earning them hundreds of thousands of dollars a year in deals that you skillfully closed. When you begin to realize this line of work doesn't fulfill you and is draining your energy. You realize that you don't agree with the business practices you have been participating in and feel like you're selling your soul for a paycheck. You ask yourself "why would I continue this work?" You may be less proactive and productive, leading your peers to question what's going on with you. You don't have an answer. Only questions at this stage, like "why am I doing this" and "what's the point?"

Phase 2: Grieving the Loss of Identity

This phase of the Dark Night comes with the realization that what you have been devoted to, who you have been committed to and what you have invested yourself in actually doesn't reflect who you are and it feels like a part of yourself has died. These old structures that you have spent so much time building, acquiring and impressing no longer matter and that can feel devastating.

For example, you can't shake the feeling that you've wasted your life, time, money and energy on chasing pursuits that don't satisfy you. You feel the void within is more pronounced than ever and you are highly aware of how empty the life that you've created actually feels. You feel like you are at a loss.

Phase 3: Disconnection / Isolation

At this stage, you completely disconnect yourself from all of the things that you have placed value on before that no longer resonate with you. You see how unfulfilling your pursuits have been so you remove yourself from participating in and maintaining these areas that feel false to you now. This may feel like the lowest point in your journey because you are exhausted from putting in so much effort towards things that don't support your soul and you don't even know where to go from here.

Depending on the person, you may reach lower lows than others. You may stay in this negative space, floating in a void for longer than the next person. You may take actions that blow up your entire life because you are so desperate to discontinue and get away from anything you don't believe in anymore. There is no set time limit on how long you spend in each phase. This journey is a personal one.

For example, you stop showing up for work. You no longer care about the relationship you're in. You stop trying to make other people happy. You cancel plans with friends. You don't return phone calls. You distance yourself and spend more time in isolation where you may entertain negative thoughts and more feelings of grief as you process your changing reality.

Phase 4: Resignation and Asking for Guidance

This phase is when you get to a point of surrender. You have realized so much that it feels like your life is a betrayal to your true self and you have no idea how to fix it and make it better. You completely resign yourself to the whim of the Universe and open yourself to help, guidance and inspiration from somewhere you may not have turned to before, like God or unseen spiritual forces.

Essentially what is happening in this phase is you have been existing in and exploring the darkness. The void. You may have been living as if you are an island, all on your own. Trying to do things on your own. Feeling as if it's all up to you to figure out. By submitting to Higher forces, you are asking for the Light to come in to the darkness and light the way. Now that you have disconnected from your old false persona, you are able to reconnect to the inner knowing that there is more to this world than meets the eye. You begin to open your heart, even if it's ever so slightly, to welcome in the benevolent love of the Universe and step into your divine line that connects you to Source, God.

For example, after distancing yourself from everything that you know as familiar, you no longer feel like you have a purpose or a direction. Being in a place of depleted energy, resources and finances, you reach an emotional moment of despair, crying out to the skies and yelling "I give up. Now what do I do? Where am I supposed to go from here? Help me! Show me. Guide me. I need help."

Phase 5: The Light Comes In

The final phase of the Dark Night is when the Light comes back in to your life. You feel the warmth of Universal love and an inkling of hope where not all is lost.

This manifests as many different things as it will be personal to each person so that it is undeniably received. Intuitive bread crumbs that I call "golden nuggets" are placed on your path to strike a cord within your being that you inherently know are guidance. Following these bread crumbs will lead you closer and closer to discovering your true self, which you can then begin to anchor into your reality resulting in a life that reflects your inner being more fully.

For example, now that you've pleaded with God to help you, you begin to notice number synchronicities appearing to you through out the day. Song titles and lyrics get your attention and feel undeniably relevant to your life. People may say things to you that ring an internal intuitive bell of recognition and the information is helpful like a guiding light. Conversely, things that are not meant to be in your life will naturally and effortlessly fall away.

Moving through the Dark Night of the Soul is an intensive life review where you have the opportunity to assess your entire life and discover your soul's truth more fully. When you allow yourself to submit to the process and take the plunge into the unknown of how things will unfold, you have the opportunity to gain insight into your life's path, soul purpose, and infinite potentialities available to you.

This process is not for the faint of heart. If your soul has chosen to go through this process, you can rest easy knowing that you are here on Earth to be and do great things. Your presence in this world has a huge impact and you are a powerful creator capable of designing a life for yourself that feels fulfilling, joyful and a direct match for your core truth. How exhilarating is that?!

Now get ready to live your life's special mission!

Reading List!

If you'd like more information on the process of depression as a means to spiritual awakening, here are some books you can check out:

1. *Dark Nights of the Soul: A Guide to Finding Your Way Through Life's Ordeals, Thomas Moore*
2. *The Dark Night of the Soul: A Psychiatrist Explores the Connection Between Darkness and Spiritual Growth, Gerald May MD*

WEEK 3

INFLUENCE – UNDERSTANDING YOUR ENERGY

Understanding your energy is the key to becoming an empowered empath. If you do not understand your energy, there is no way that you will be able to manage your energy and thus will continue to be drained, depleted, or worse, become ill. One of the biggest contributors that keeps an empath disconnected from truly understanding yourself is the impact of influence on your energy.

Everywhere you go in this world, there is something clamoring for your energy, attempting to influence you. Whether it be from advertisements popping up on your screen, commercials on the radio, sales people at the store, your children running circle around you, codependent parents, one-sided relationships or needy friendships, your energy is constantly in demand! "Give me your attention!" "Give me your time!" "Spend your money here!" "I need you now!"

This is simply an energetic reality of this world. I want you to think of this world like a video game, for a moment. Imagine you are playing a character with a mission to complete the level with your energy in tact, but there are characters that pop up without warning that you need to dodge in order to protect your energy. Now you understand the plight of the empath!

We will talk more about how to protect and shield yourself from these solicitors of your energy in Week 6: Insulate. For now, we are going to discuss where to begin and how to set yourself up for success.

Step 1: Establish a Sanctuary

The very first requirement for all empaths to set themselves up for success is to make a space that's all your own. This needs to be a space that is just for you and you *ONLY*. Even if you are living with a large family, it is essential that you are able to carve out a place that is undisturbed by others.

Ideally, this would be an entire room all to yourself like an office or meditation studio. Some of you are lucky enough to have a lot of space to yourself already, so for you it would be easier to manage the energy and boundaries of that space.

For others of you, it may be more of a challenge to find a special place to call your own. In this case, if you are struggling to figure out how to do this, I would recommend that you have a desk or a comfortable chair in the home that everyone understands and agrees is just for you. No one will put their mail or dirty laundry in your space. If the other residents of the home see you are at your desk or in your chair, you are not to be disturbed. You can also amplify this signal by putting on headphones when you are in this space.

This space is meant to be your safe zone. No distractions. No disruptions. No chaotic energy interfering with your peaceful place. If you live with others, then it must be understood that you need undisturbed time. They must wait for you to be available before interacting with you. If it can't wait, they must knock before entering your space. You are not to be diverted from the task you set out to do in your space, whether it be journaling, meditation, paying bills or simply twiddle your thumbs while staring at the walls. This is your sanctuary to do whatever you will.

Step 2: Spend Time Alone

Spending time alone as an empath cannot be underestimated. The importance of seeking solace within your own energy is crucial to the overall wellness and balance of the empath. This is imperative for all empaths to spend time alone in order to regenerate energy supplies but also get a clear understanding of what your energy feels like.

Some people are more prone to seek this out naturally. Others may find it is difficult to break away from the daily grind or the demanding needs of others to seek alone time.

If you are new to spending time alone, it may be extremely uncomfortable to begin. Your mind may feel restless. You may feel anxious. You may have uncomfortable thoughts or memories constantly running through your mind. You may experience impulses to check your phone or turn on some sort of distraction like the tv or a video game. You may think of all the things you need to get done.

This is all ok and does not need to be judged. You're not doing it wrong. The point of spending time alone is to get familiar with your own energetic signature

Your energetic signature is like the frequency fingerprint of your own soul. If you are living a life of constant distraction and influence, you may not have a clear understanding of what your energetic signature actually feels like. When left alone, you may be even more aware of how statically charged your energy actually is.

When you don't have a firm grasp on your own energetic signature, you may have thoughts and feelings that do not originate from yourself, yet you may think they belong to you because you don't know how to differentiate between the energies yet.

Understanding your energy will serve you as you become more clear over time in the sense that you can quickly identify and discern what thoughts, ideas, people, places or opportunities are not for you. This will become much easier once you learn how to clear your energy, which we will discuss in the next section. Firstly, it's important to find a safe place where you can open up your energy centers and practice tuning into your natural energetic signature.

You can begin by clearing your mind as much as possible. Observe the thoughts, feelings or questions that float into your mind and release them to your angels for safe keeping.

If you find this to be very challenging, you can do a "brain dump" of everything that is in your mind until you feel like it's empty. You can journal or even make a list to get it all out of your head. You can come back to it later, but for now, the goal is to empty your mind, When you find that you are reaching for anything to add to your brain dump, you're in a good place to begin tuning into your energy.

Set aside time each day to sit in your sanctuary and tune in to your energetic signature. Try this for a whole week and take note of how you feel each day. Complete one full week of this practice before moving on to the next week.

How do you feel each day in your sanctuary?

- Day 1: _____
- Day 2: _____
- Day 3: _____
- Day 4: _____
- Day 5: _____
- Day 6: _____
- Day 7: _____

Step 3: Energy Clearing

Now that you are aware of how many external energetic factors can influence and impact your energy, it is important to clear your energy as much as possible before you do anything else. Before entering into any energy activities, it is of the highest importance to clear your energy and the energy of your environment first.

In an effort to open up your energy, you must avoid inhibiting substances that are designed to keep you in a state of numbness and a lower form of consciousness. By abstaining from the following, you are systematically reversing any desensitization conditioning that was meant to negatively influence your awareness and ultimately keep your vibration low.

Avoid the following:

- Horror movies
- Fail videos or shock tv
- Public radio stations
- Mainstream news
- Caffeine
- Alcohol
- Chemicals
- Pharmaceuticals
- Natural flavor as an ingredient
- Unfiltered tap water
- Highly processed and fast food
- Cigarettes
- Fluoride toothpaste
- Loud sound systems in home or vehicle
- Environments with lots of yelling/shouting

Which of these can you give up right now?

_____

_____

_____

_____

In partnership with avoiding certain toxic factors, you can take proactive steps to actively clear your energy and raise your vibration. There are many different methods of clearing the energy of your aura and environment.

Experiment with the following methods to clear your energy. Check off each one as you try it.

- Smudge with smoke using incense or healing herbs such as sage, Palo Santo, juniper, sweet grass, Yerba Santa, cedar, copal, lavendar, frankincense, etc.
- Hold, wear or work with Selenite, a stone that never needs to be cleansed as it emanates an angelic frequency into the user and environment that it is in.
- Take a shower or epsom salt bath to wash away energetic debris.
- Create a crystal grid in your sanctuary using protective crystals such as Black Tourmaline.
- Call in Divine Source light such a white light or the Violet Flame to enter your space and your energy, clearing away all energetic residue, density and cutting all cords that do not serve you.
- Listen to a guided meditation or Solfeggio frequencies for energy clearing.
- Use an activated spray such as Rose Water or liquid sage to cleanse yourself and your space.
- Use bells, chimes or singing bowls to emit cleansing tones into your energy and environment.
- Sit in a circle of sea salt, this may get messy but salt is often used in ritual as a cleansing and protection agent.
- Open the windows in your space to welcome in fresh air.
- Pay attention to the Feng Shui and flow of chi in your

space by hanging mirrors or rearranging furniture.

- Clean yourself or your environment. Whenever you tidy up or deep clean, you are moving energy and raising the vibration through your focused intention and care.
- Clear your body and open your channel by detoxing from processed foods. Anything that has been processed, genetically modified, manipulated and altered has a deafening effect on your body's natural frequency and flow, so cut the junk out of your diet and eat as clean as possible.
- Smile! Every time you smile, you let the light in. When you smile, know that it's healthy for you and don't conceal it. Embrace it. Notice what makes you smile. Pay attention. Write it down. Over time, you will be able to thread together a theme of what truly brings you joy and happiness. Use that as your divine compass to guide you forward in your life. In your decision making. In your emotions. In your perspective. In your vibration.

Which methods did you enjoy doing the most and will continue in your practice?

_____

_____

_____

Step 4: Exercises for Energy Management

Once you have established an intention of clearing and cleansing your energy, you are safe to begin opening up your energy field. Start by playing with your energy to see what is possible and what it feels like when you direct your attention to certain possibilities.

Flex Your Aura:

One idea is to tune into your energy field and envision your aura like a bubble of light around your body.

Push out the bubble of light and suck it back in. Push it out again and suck it back in. Do this a number of times. Change the speed in which you flex your aura, faster than slowly.

Feel into the difference. Get an idea of what you are experiencing just playing with your energy without any external influences affecting you.

What do you notice?

_____

_____

_____

Energy Flush:

This exercise may be easier if you record your own voice reading the prompts and then listen back with headphones while you do the exercise with your eyes closed.

Sit in a comfortable position and bring your awareness down to your feet. Imagine your feet have tendrils and roots coming out of your soles.

Watch as these roots penetrate into the floor, into the Earth, traveling further down into the ground and connecting into the earth grid energy. When you feel the roots have connected into the Earth grid, inhale to pull energy up from the Earth into your system, as if you are drinking in the energy through a straw.

Take 3 full deep breaths and call upon all of your energy to return home to you.

Bring your awareness to the top of your head. Feel your crown start to tingle, open and signal to your spiritual support team to join you: God, Higher self, Ascended masters, Archangels, Spirit guides, Guardian beings of a Higher realm.

As you feel their presence around you, focus on strengthening your energetic boundaries. Feel how safe and secure you are in your own energy.

Ask your energy where are the soft spots in my aura that need attention? You might see it in your minds eye. You might feel an itch or tingly sensations on your body. Watch as these soft spots strengthen and fill with divine Source light.

As you feel your auric field and psychic shield getting stronger, watch as your spiritual support is removing all cords and energetic hooks from your field. Parasites, implants, energetic debris, psychic attacks and residual energy that do not belong to you are all removed at this time.

Watch as this denser energy is bundled and sent back to Divine Source to be transmuted into something neutral or positive, causing no harm to others in your release.

Bring your awareness back down to your feet as you anchor into your shifted shiny vibration. Your energy is radiant and glowing! Squeaky clean!

When you're ready, gently open your eyes.

Quick and Dirty Clearing:

This technique is useful for when you are on the go or don't have the time or space to dedicate to a deeper flush, but need a quick reset in the moment.

Clasp both hands over your solar plexus and close your eyes. When you close your eyes and hands like this, you are closing your energy circuit so that you are in your own energy and not open to anyone or anything else, but rather focused on your own vibration.

Repeat three times out loud or to yourself (incantations are always more powerful out loud) "I release all energy that is not mine. I release all energy that is not mine. I release all energy that is not mine."

Take a deep breath. "And so it is."

Notice, how do you feel now?

W E E K   4

IMPLANT – GROUNDING

The idea of grounding, or being grounded, has many facets. Often times there can be a negative connotation, like when teenagers get grounded by their parents or when flights are grounded and won't arrive on time. But when you're an empath, being grounded is not only desirable, it is yet another essential part of your overall energetic management. Ideally, empaths need to keep their intentions firmly implanted in Earth energy.

Step 1: Identify Being Ungrounded

When an empath is ungrounded, accidents can happen. Bad decisions can be made. Details are overlooked. Anxiety can be induced. Feelings get hurt. Opportunities are missed. Relationships, finances and overall health can suffer. People can regard you as an insensitive or careless person when you're really not. You're just not grounded.

Also, if you are an empath who struggles to cope with painful realities or has suffered trauma, this can literally catapult your consciousness out of the body. Especially if you suffered from trauma early on in life and have not yet processed, released, or healed this trauma, your consciousness may be in the habit of spending most of it's time outside of the body, making it nearly impossible to stay grounded without effort.

I have also encountered many starseed empaths who's consciousness exists in 2 or more different places at all times. Although it's true, we are all multidimensional beings and exist in many places at once, these souls I'm referring to, however, tend to be older souls with higher dimensional roots and intense life lessons. It is as if their consciousness is constantly plugged in to a higher intelligence to continuously stream higher wisdom into this world. These are often the souls that have the most challenges with living on Earth in the sense that paying bills, managing time or remembering to eat can easily elude them. Can you relate?

Ways to know when you're not grounded:

- Constantly multi-tasking and never fully present
- Clumsy, bumping into things, dropping things, easily injuring yourself
- Feeling spacey, constantly zoning out
- Hard to focus, short attention span, easily distracted
- Feeling overwhelmed by options, unable to make a decision
- Being scattered, starting things without finishing them
- Caught up in other people's crises, dramas or emergencies
- You're late a lot or miss appointments, meetings and deadlines

- No follow through on things you say you will do
- Extra emotional or easily triggered
- Fall asleep during meditation but not at bedtime because your mind is racing
- Hard to hold a conversation because you jump from topic to topic rapidly or lose your train of thought

You can see how being in an ungrounded state can negatively impact your life, career, relationships, and even health. It may also negatively influence your confidence and opinion of yourself where you may be telling yourself you'e not good at certain things, when you may actually just need to get grounded.

Step 2: How to Get Grounded

Grounding refers to rooting yourself so you feel stable, connected and balanced. It involves connecting with the Earth grid, or Crystalline grid of energy, which is always running pure Earth energy. It also refers to being fully present in the body, directing your energy in the moment. Remaining in the here and now.

When we live such a demanding, fast-paced life filled with constant distractions and encounter so many interfering energies, we can often be separated from our energetic anchor points.

Fortunately, we are given the tools to easily reconnect into stability and ground ourselves.

Experiment with the following ways to ground your energy. Check them off as you try each method:

- Spending time outdoors like hiking, picnicking, gardening, and camping
- Living in tune with nature's rhythms, such as eating seasonally, waking up with the sunrise or doing a polar bear plunge
- Visualization techniques, grounding meditations, setting intention
- Earthing, walking barefoot in the earth or sticking your naked feet into the dirt, sand or water
- Exercise, moving your body puts you back into your physical form
- Volunteer to support the Earth, local ranger station, trash pickup
- Ground through food such as red meat, root vegetables
- Work with grounding crystals such as aragonite, polychrome jasper, hematite, petrified wood, red jasper, copper turquoise, etc.
- Burning sandalwood, patchouli or bay leaves
- Eliminating in nature (aka peeing in the woods)
- Working with mud or clay such as sculpting, mud mask or mud baths

Which methods did you enjoy doing most and will continue in your practice?

_____

_____

_____

It is advisable to make this a regular practice and ground frequently as a part of your own self care. You can use these techniques to ground in the moment or choose to live a more grounded lifestyle. The beauty part about grounding is that it can easily adapt to all lifestyles. Whether you work in a busy office building and take time to eat your lunch outside in the sunshine, or you live in the mountains and spend most of your days cooking burgers while barefoot outside, there is room for grounding in all of our lives. It's up to you to make the effort.

Step 3: Exercise for Grounding

Grounding Visualization:

This technique is another one that would be best if you record your own voice and listen back to it with your eyes closed. The more you do it, the more familiar you will become with the steps so you won't always need the recording.

Bring your awareness to your feet. Focus on the chakras at the bottom-center of your feet, in the middle of your arches. Visualize these chakras lighting up with white light as they activate.

Next imagine your feet and legs are turning into trees trunks that are rooting deeply into into the Earth.

As you firmly plant your roots into the earth, bring your awareness to the base of your spine. This is where your root chakra resides. Visualize this chakra lighting up with intense red light as it activates.

Witness a cord extending out of your root chakra like a tail and extending down into the subterranean layers of the Earth.

Watch as this cord travels to the center of the Earth to find the core of the Earth, made of molten iron, spinning and churning with life.

Observe the cord from your root chakra coiling around the center of the Earth and returning back up to you, landing back in your root chakra.

Breathe deeply as you inhale this molten Earth energy and receive it as nourishment for your body and energy field.

Stay in this feeling as long as feels necessary. Feel your body relax, your shoulders drop, your heart soften. Feel your nervous system calm itself and your breathing regulate and stabilize.

Send pulses of gratitude though your feet roots and root chakra cord to the Earth. Feel her send you love in return.

Open your eyes and notice the shift that has taken place in your body. Your energy will be more calm. Your eyesight might be more clear.

Move slowly onto your next task and focus on one thing at a time to maintain this grounded state.

WEEK 5

IGNITE —
ACTIVATING YOUR ENERGY

Activating your energy is what ignites your personal power! It will allow you to use, balance and manage your own energetic life force to serve you as you move through your life.

It's important to understand the many ways in which energy moves through your system and how to interact with it. Since energy is a truly awesome fact of nature that carries divine traits by nature, the possibilities of how to activate, balance and work with your energy are infinite — and completely up to you to explore! However, we will discuss a few fundamental principles to establish as a baseline for you to build upon.

Step 1: Bodies of Consciousness

As you exist in all forms, you are made up entirely of vibrations and frequency. While incarnated in human form, our soul's conscious awareness resides in multiple areas known as bodies of consciousness. This allows humans to experience and process energy in a multitude of ways.

These bodies of consciousness include (but are not limited to): spiritual body, causal body, astral body, mental body, emotional body, physical body.

Spiritual Body:

The spirit body or light body is often considered the spark of your soul. This body cannot be created nor destroyed as it is pure god source energy.

Causal Body:

This body of consciousness can be likened to the higher self or monad and remains connected to the individual persona at all times. This body is connected to the Akashic Records, storing and recording all karmic records. It has no absolute location as it exists in all realms, making humans multidimensional in existence.

Astral Body:

In this body, your consciousness is able to experience the dream realm, navigate different dimensions and travel through space and time. Remote viewers and long-distance psychics utilize this body of consciousness most often when accessing information.

Mental Body:

This is the body of consciousness responsible for your stream of thought, the ability to engage in logical conversations, plan things methodically, approach situations pragmatically (ideally). It is connected to the physical body in the sense that the physical brain and body function can influence the mental body and vice versa. Mind over matter.

Emotional Body:

This center of experience is where you are able to feel your emotions and interpret the energy that is in motion (e-motion = energy in motion). You process a lot of energy in this body of consciousness. Empaths often have a highly sensitized emotional body, even if underdeveloped.

Physical Body:

This body is our physical, corporal body. The vehicle you use to move through physical life.

The thing to be aware of is how there is a trickle down effect when it comes to your bodies of consciousness. If you are ignoring or neglecting energetic information in your spiritual body, it will spill over to your causal body. Not many unmanaged empaths have an awareness that this body even exists, so you may experience that neglected energy carrying over into your astral body. This is where dreams are repeatedly trying to communicate the energy held within the subconscious. If nothing is done to fully process the energy in the astral body, it will show up in your emotional body. You may start feeling sad, anxious or depressed but unable to identify the cause. If this is allowed to continue without clearing, the energy that spills over into your mental body. You may become overwhelmed, flooded with thoughts and self doubt. Finally, if you cannot make sense of what you are experiencing, the energy will ultimately land and collect in your physical body, which I like to call "the loudest messenger." If you have not gotten the message that your spirit has been trying to tell you, you will end up experiencing locked energy within your physical body. This may manifest as pain, injury, illness or even limited mobility.

Step 2: Learn the Chakras

Chakras are the spinning energy centers within your human energy body. They process, carry, hold and store specific energies as well as connects you to infinite wisdom and resources.

Your chakras can be active or inactive. Balanced and unbalanced. Clear or completely blocked. Energy is constantly moving and changing so it is understandable that our chakras are in a constant state of fluctuation and adjustment as well! Fortunately you have the ability to focus your attention on these energy centers and work with them to manage your own energy.

Most people are familiar with the initial 7 chakras that enable you to interact with and navigate the 3rd dimensional physical realm. Since human beings are multidimensional, you also have chakras that exist in higher dimensions. There are countless energy portals and points among the human bodies of consciousness, but for the sake of this book, we will discuss 22 chakras.

3rd Dimensional Chakras

1. Root: I AM.

Location — Base of spine, pelvic floor

Color — Red

Function — How you are existing in the physical realm, clothing self, feeding self, money, shelter, feeling safe, strong sense of morals and values, trusting your surroundings, feeling capable of thriving, foundation in this world. Slowest moving chakra, holds the most dense energy of all chakras.

Issues — Money issues, financial blockages, issues finding stable housing, feeling unsafe or unstable, easily triggered fight or flight response, lacking direction, avoiding life responsibilities, dominating, bullying, egocentric, issues with anus or rectum, autoimmune issues, adrenal fatigue, eating disorders.

2. Sacral: I FEEL.

Location — Below the navel, over the reproductive organs

Color — Orange

Function — How you feel and interpret things, how do you receive the world, sexual energy, creative center, kundalini rests within this chakra, relationships to other people, romance, family, partnership, feeling center, seed of desires such as desire to learn, explore, experience life, pleasure the senses, independence, ecstacy.

Issues — Not trusting compliments or love directed your way, one bad relationship after another, attracting unhealthy or controlling people or situations, promiscuity, sex addictions, sex aversions, inability to enjoy pleasures simple or otherwise, repression, fear of intimacy, hip issues, reproductive problems, infertility, menstrual issues.

3. Solar Plexus: I DO.

Location — Between navel and solar plexus

Color — Yellow

Function — How you present yourself to the world, your confidence, discipline, wisdom, will power, self-assured, confidence, ability to infuse confidence in others, curious, charisma, what messages you send out into the world, this is where your inner fire lives.

Issues — Low self esteem, victim mentality, feeling like the world is against you, feel like things are being done to you not for you, lacking confidence or ability to express passion, procrastinating, lying to self, living in denial, overly critical, fear of being alone, no trust in own judgement, stomach issues, hernias, IBS, adrenal imbalance, colon disease, pancreas issues.

4. Heart: I LOVE.

Location — Middle of chest

Color — Green

Function — Making emotionally-based decisions, communicating through heart center, joy, compassion, ability to connect with those who can't communicate for themselves like animals and children, oneness, interconnectedness, relatability, happy, feeling loved and cared for, generous, charitable.

Issues — Lacking trust, fearing being hurt, avoiding repeat of past negative events, sad, not open to new love or opportunity, carrying grief, draining energy by helping others, compensating by being overly joyful or inauthentically sincere, heart disease, breast issues, high blood pressure, respiratory issues, upper back tension, arm injury.

5. Throat: I SPEAK.

Location — Throat center

Color — Sky blue

Function — Where your truth is all to be expressed, seen and understand, how you are able to communicate, ability to say what you want when you want using words of love and kindness, personal expression, a clear sense of who you are and how you want to be seen.

Issues — Not speaking up, saying yes when you mean no, repressing your feelings, lying, deception, scared to communicate, keeping secrets, feeling misunderstood, not allowed to communicate openly, stiff neck, sore throat, chronic cough, thyroid imbalance, esophageal injury, teeth issues, gum disease, mouth problems, speech impediment.

6. Third Eye: I SEE.

Location — Center of forehead

Color — Indigo blue

Function — The energy center that allows you to see where you're going on your path, able to view what is aligned or supportive, assists in discernment, the watch tower of the energy system that can see things coming a mile away, interprets information that cannot be seen by the naked eye, intuition, strategy, observant, perceptive.

Issues — Blindsided by shocking news or events, doubting your own intuition, biased or limited perspective, forgetful, jealous, rejection of spirituality or energetic influence, brain dysfunction, nerves system issues, eye problems, ear infections.

7. Crown: I UNDERSTAND.

Location — Top center of skull

Color — Violet purple

Function — Enables you to open up and connect with God, divine love, all-that-is, centering within divine line, receive psychic information or higher dimensional downloads, empathic abilities, compassion, deep understanding that God exists in all things, everything is connected.

Issues — Self-centered, self focused, easily bored, feeling completely lost in life, being cut off from love for God, atheism, migraines or chronic head ache, depression, isolation, skin issues, chronic fatigue, skeletal disease.

4th Dimensional Chakras

Before accessing and working with your higher dimensional chakras (or outer chakras), it's important to work with the first 7 chakras to ensure they are balanced and activated. Once you become familiar with the initial 7 chakras within the 3D realm, you may then find more accessibility when connecting to 4th dimensional chakras, thus enabling you to move further into the 5th dimensional chakras.

While working with the 4th dimensional chakra system, this is where you will explore how you are able to interact with and affect change within the 4th dimension, also known as space and time, in a timeless and formless being.

8. High Heart: Soul Star

Location — A foot above the head

Color — Turquoise

Function — A bridge between 3rd dimension and 4th, connects to the causal body of consciousness that carries past life memories, karmic records, natural abilities, inherent preferences, like and dislikes, seat of the soul resides here.

Issues — Past life trauma affecting this lifetime, energetic blockages carried over from past life experiences, karmic debt, phobias from traumatic soul experiences, ailments in physical body derived from past life wounds.

9. Atomic Doorway:

Location — Approximately 10 inches above High Heart chakra

Color — Kelly green

Function — Houses your soul blueprint that comprises your 3rd dimensional chakra system as well as highly detailed information about your soul, the gateway to the Akashic Records, check point for alignment, psychic and healing abilities from other lifetimes are stored here to be accessed when aligned, pure soul truth unaffected by ego or agenda, energy center for communication and communion with alternate life such as extraterrestrial species.

Issues — Access may be blocked, unable to tap into psychic abilities, fearful of psychic abilities.

10. Solar Star:

Location — Approximately 1 foot beneath your feet

Color — White, pearlescent

Function — Grounds the abilities that you have stored in your soul records that you have developed and acquired in past evolutionary souls cycles, enables you to tap into and develop psychic skillset in this lifetime, not only access abilities but develop, strengthen and control them. If you are aware that you are involved in a Twin Flame dynamic and walking the path of the Twin Flame journey, you can assume you are working within this chakra center.

Issues — Imbalance or total division of Divine Masculine and Divine Feminine energies within energy system, cannot access full potential until these energies are harmonized working through the heart chakra as the access point in the 3rd dimension, Twin Flame journey in separation.

11. Galactic:

Location — Palm of right hand

Color — Coral, pink orange

Function — Connects to the Divine will of the individual working through the personal power center within the 3rd dimensional solar plexus chakra, this enables one to manifest and bring intention through to physical creation, inspired action, telekinesis, telemetry, pyrokinesis, weaving higher dimensional wisdom into form.

Issues — Manifestation blockages, inability to create or act upon ideas, unable to access this chakra due to trauma in lower chakras, manifestations result in distorted version of intention.

12. Earth Star:

Location — Palm of left hand

Color — Glittery gold

Function — Connects to Christ consciousness, works with monad, receives information from Higher self, keeps one open to observation through complete detachment and receptivity, enables one to view circumstance without the influence of emotions, ego or attachment, neutral assessment.

Issues — If one is closed off and energetically in a state of 'no' then one would not be able to receive a higher perspective through this chakra, standing too close to an issue, missing bigger picture.

13. Universal Mother: Earth Core

Location — Approximately a foot in front of physical body

Color — Magenta, deep rose

Function — This chakra vibrates at the resonance of pure, unadulterated unconditional divine love, healing frequency is always available immediately in front of you, literally, as long as you open yourself up to let in the infinite abundance of love, always present, always.

Issues — By design, this chakra is never blocked, only our awareness of it can be blocked.

14. Universal Sun: I KNOW.

Location — Known as the higher octave of the third eye chakra

Color — Deep violet

Function — When one steps out of the monkey mind and ego, this is where one would "step into," disengages the chatter so the Divine plan can be perceived, clairsentience, acceptance of divine order, all knowing.

Issues — Experiencing delsuions, hearing voices that are harmful, telling you to do bad things, senility, dementia, paranoia, neuroses.

15. Universal Father:

Location — Deep space

Color — Pale magenta, soft gold white

Function — Portal to ascension, this is the gateway that leads to expansion of consciousness, elevates out of the lower density worlds and becomes out of reach for any lower vibrational energies to attach, influence or infect, energetically untouchable to lower worlds.

Issues — Either this portal chakra is accessible or it is not. You can gain access to this chakra portal by moving through the previous chakras, allowing you access to the higher 5th dimensional chakras.

5th Dimensional Chakras

When working with the 5th dimensional chakras, it is important to remember that there is no physical form in the 5th dimension and therefore cannot validate the true purpose, location or existence of these chakras. It is up to you to truly explore what these energy centers mean to you.

The following information is a combination of inspiration from Elizabeth Ashley's work as well as my own experience-derived theory. My goal in sharing this information with you is to give you a target to aim your focus and work on expanding that through your own spiritual explorations and creative pursuits. May this information serve as a vehicle for you to make your own discoveries!

16. Spiritual Ascension:

Color — Soft violet white

Function — The decision chakra, one can liken this to the pearly gates of heaven, only the sovereign soul is making the judgement (not St. Peter) to stay within the realms of denser form or to rise into a higher vibrational existence, majority of souls who go through near death experiences gather into this chakra once leaving the physical body in order to make their ultimate decision; to transition over or to return to life on earth. This is also the chakra in which spontaneous ascension occurs where an individual transcends from physical form and moves into their light body through activation of this chakra. It is possible to work with this chakra, decide to stay in physical form and continue on to work with the higher chakras succeeding this one.

17. Universal Light:

Color — White

Function — Completely disconnected from ego, instinct, and agenda, an infinite space of existence, establishes an all-knowing, access to all information, existing outside of time and space, simultaneous existence of everything that has ever been and ever will be ad infinitum.

18. Divine Intention:

Color — Golden rose

Function — I call this chakra "the psychic switchboard" as this is the portal enabling one to connect with and channel ascended masters and higher dimensional beings, bringing their wisdom and guidance through multiple dimensions and grounding it in the 3rd dimension, think Abraham Hicks or Bashar.

19. Great Cosmic Heartbeat:

Color — Magenta

Function — The energy center where a soul is able to disconnect completely from all earthly and physical connections, cords, memories and attachments, supported solely by the unconditional love and bliss of the Godhead, moving into the ultimate freedom of existence. This is the chakra point most souls move through after transitioning (death) but you do not have to die in order to connect and work with this energy center.

20. Co-Creator with the Divine:

Color — Golden violet

Function — This energy center is the total awareness of your consciousness acting as an extension of the Divine, the purpose to create thorough existence, communication occurs purely using the frequency of unconditional love, being for the sake of being.

21. Divine Cellular Structure:

Color — Golden blue

Function — Your consciousness becomes in on the Divine plan, as far as knowing, seeing, understanding, being the all-knowing and simultaneously playing a role in the creation of form through vibration and frequency, you are both the creator and the creation at once.

22. Celestial:

Color — Platinum

Function — A higher octave of the 3rd dimensional crown chakra existing in the 5th dimension, the connection point to angelic frequencies and angels.

Step 3: Raise Your Vibration

You are the captain of your own energy ship and you have the ability to command your own energy. This includes the ability to raise your vibration at will! And in a world that solely exists based on vibration and frequency, the vibe that you are holding and emanating plays an all-encompassing role in how your life experience unfolds before you.

Although it may sound like a complication notion, all it takes is a little bit of self awareness and a few energy tricks stored up your sleeve. Let's try a few exercises to get you warmed up to raising your vibration.

Emotional Scale

Just like we went over in Week 1, use your emotions as an indicator for where your vibration is currently. Check in with yourself right now. What are the dominant emotions you are feeling right now?

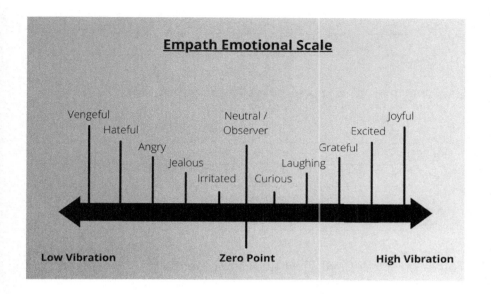

Empath Emotional Scale

If you notice you are lower on the emotional scale, such as feeling sad, hopeless, regretful or depressed, the easiest way to shift your vibration is to take a small, manageable action that will begin to lift your frequency level.

Stepping into gratitude is an easy one because you can start with something small. Begin by thinking of something simple that you are grateful for like having a meal today or being able to clean your body regularly. If you really give yourself a minute to sit and think, you can easily come up with 5 things to be grateful for. Then maybe once you list out those 5 things, you can think of another 5 things that bring you joy. Finish up by coming up with another 5 things that make you smile!

Gratitude List:

1. _____
2. _____
3. _____

4. _____

5. _____

Can you think of 5 more things to be grateful for?

6. _____

7. _____

8. _____

9. _____

10. _____

You're on a roll now! How about another 5?

11. _____

12. _____

13. _____

14. _____

15. _____

Did you notice yourself smiling as you completed this list?

Although this is usually the most simple way to begin shifting out of negative emotions and slowly build momentum, sometimes the low vibe is just too strong and the monkey mind will try to keep pulling you down. The good news is there are additional ways of managing your vibration and reclaiming control.

Shifting Focus

Another technique to shift your vibration is to literally take your mind off of whatever is making you feel the lower vibrational emotions and focus on something more positive. An example of this might be if you're having a bad day at work or you are arguing with your partner, these are situations that can make you feel angry or agitated and you might want to try to fix the situation immediately. Or worse, you may want to retaliate in the heat of the moment!

Rather than trying to fix the problem, don't make a move without first shifting your energy. You might decide to watch videos of puppies being cute on the internet or a stand up comedy routine to get you laughing a bit. Once you notice your emotional state has shifted, you can rest assured your vibration has shifted as well. You have just officially regained control over your own energy. It is now safe to have any difficult conversations because you are now in a much more powerful place to tackle whatever problem or issue was pulling you down earlier from a position of empowerment.

Prayer

Simply talking to God will shift your vibration. You can literally shift the vibration of things by praying over them such as bringing healing to a sick person or blessing a meal. The more you do it, the more potent and impactful it becomes, also the deeper your relationship with the divine will be.

If talking to God feels too intimidating or there's still too much resistance around that right now, that's alright. What feels closer within reach to you? Talking to angels, deceased loved ones, spirit guides or even your Higher self are all beneficial when raising your vibration. Prayer is essentially fool-proof. You can't do it wrong.

Even if you are vibrationally at an all time low and you are just completely exasperated by life, holding a super negative vibration and at a point of desperation (like during the Dark Night of the Soul covered in Week 2), simply opening yourself up to any higher guidance or help from a higher source of energy will be enough to make a difference in your vibration.

Remember the 18th chakra, the Universal Mother. You have a chakra that is ever present, inches in front of you, at all times. You are never without a portal to tap into unconditional divine source love. Prayer, speaking words of intention, calling upon the light, all have a profound effect on your overall frequency by opening your energy enough to receive the love that is always there, ever present.

Give it a try right now. Close your eyes and call upon a trusted energy such as God or your higher self. Speak directly to this power and don't be afraid to hold back. Watch what pours out of you once you really get going and allow yourself to surrender into prayer and speak freely.

Breathwork

For anyone just beginning meditation, you may be taught to focus your attention on your breath. If your mind wanders, simply return your attention to your breath. Always return to your breath.

There is good reason for this. Breathwork is a powerful gateway to tapping in to and controlling your super powers as you can direct the flow of energy by directing the flow of your breath.

You may be familiar with the infamous "Iceman" Wim Hof who can submerge himself in Arctic waters for minutes at a time only to surface unscathed and refreshed. He has performed miraculous feats that most people would never even dream are possible because of his masterful breath work and meditative skills. Fortunately he is also widely known for teaching people how to do what he can do by hacking into their primary and secondary nervous systems. All of this is achieved simply by mastering breathing techniques in conjunction with additional exercises.

Developing a regular practice of breathwork has many advantages since the flow of our energy affects all aspects of our lives. Breathwork has been credited as restoring health, moving trauma from and through the body, opening energy centers and more.

Here are a few benefits of breathwork:

- Calms anxiety
- Alleviates fear
- Shifts you out of depression
- Processes grief
- Soothes anger
- Reduces stress
- Releases emotional, mental and physical trauma
- Boosts immunity
- Increases feelings of joy, happiness and openness
- Develops self awareness
- Improves confidence and self-image
- Strengthens lung capacity
- Raises vibration!

A simple exercise that you can try right now is an exercise known as 4-7-8 breathing. In this exercise, you will breathe in to the count of 4. Hold for the count of 7. Exhale to the count of 8. Repeat this for a total of 3 cycles. Pause your reading here and try it now.

Breathe in...2...3...4...
Hold...2...3...4...5...6...7...
Exhale...2...3...4...5...6...7...8...

Again.
Breathe in...2...3...4...
Hold...2...3...4...5...6...7...
Exhale...2...3...4...5...6...7...8...

One last time.
Breathe in...2...3...4...
Hold...2...3...4...5...6...7...
Exhale...2...3...4...5...6...7...8...
Well done! How do you feel?

_____

_____

_____

There are a variety of breathwork methods derived from different traditions and practitioners that you might like to explore:

- Chi gong
- Yogic breath / Pranayama
- Breathing meditation

- Shamanic breathwork
- Transformational breathwork
- Rebirthing
- Vivation
- Clarity breathing
- Holotropic breathwork

If you are practicing breathwork and begin to experience anything such as blurred vision, dizziness or heart palpitations, please discontinue immediately or seek the support of a trained guide.

Step 4: Methods to Ignite Energy

Now that you have learned so much about your energy centers and have an entire repertoire of options to raise your vibration, you are more in control of your energy than every before!

There really is no short supply of things you can do to engage and ignite your energy. It's just a matter of taking the steps to do it. Sometimes, all it will take is a shift in thought to raise your vibration. Other times, you may need a bit more focused intention to engage your energy in a way that really works for you.

Here is a quick reference list for some ideas of what you can do to ignite that precious energy of yours. Check them off as you try each one:

- Meditation, guided or self-directed
- Balance and heal chakras, one-by-one or full system
- Yoga, specific poses and mudras available for each chakra

- Binaural beats (listen to with headphones or ear buds only)
- Solfeggio frequencies (find for free on YouTube)
- Body movement (exercise, dancing, ecstatic, freeform)
- Essential oils (wear, diffuse, work with)
- Massage with healing herbs and oils
- Epsom salt baths
- Work with crystals (carry, wear, gridding, meditation)
- Coaching, counseling or therapy
- Sensory deprivation tanks
- Moon rituals
- Creative pursuits such as singing, painting, writing
- Tantra practices
- Power posing
- Work with a healer or energy practitioner

Which methods did you enjoy doing the most and will continue in your practice?

_____

_____

_____

The more you learn about yourself and your own energetic signature, the more familiar you will become with what works for you. You will continue to learn and develop the practices that benefit you most. You will also get faster at identifying imbalances within your energy and be able to self-correct much quicker!

When it comes to choosing what to do, there truly is no set guidelines on what to do or how to work with your own energy.

You simply enjoy the smorgasbord of options available to you and try a little bit of everything! If you don't like a certain practice or don't stick with something long-term, there's no need for judgement. You're just learning what is and is not meant for you. The things that work best and resonate most will tend to stick around in your life for a while.

Step 5: Chakra Ping-Pong

You have spent a lot of time in the 3D chakra system, so that may feel more familiar to you when you are beginning your journey. However, as you awaken, you may ping-pong from dimension to dimension as you explore, open and activate your outer chakras. The way this works is fascinating:

Say for example you have a moment that inspires a higher dimensional experience, such as being visited by a spirit guide in a dream or witnessing an extra terrestrial event. This experience changes you. It's like time stops and it feels so real. You are aware of things that you were never aware of before in ways that you would never have been able to process before. You know this is special and magical while it is happening. You also know this is occurring because of the energetic work and spiritual opening you have been doing.

The ping-pong effect comes in when you revert back to the lower matrix of doubt. You tell yourself *"No, that wasn't real. Couldn't be. That didn't really happen. I didn't just see that."* Because the mind cannot explain your experience logically, it now attempts to dismiss it and brush it off.

But you are awakening. Once you see something, you cannot unsee it. You can't put the spiritual toothpaste back in the tube! You know what you experienced was real. So you then begin to question your reality as you have always known it.

Now that you have "visited" this higher dimensional reality and had this experience of awareness, you have a point of reference to return to vibrationally. You aim your focus and set your intention to reconnect with the energy of that multidimensional experience through the memory of the experience, lifting you back up into that higher reality and existing in a higher frequency. Yes, doesn't that feel nice?

At first, you may feel a little uncertain as you go from a lower dimensional awareness up to a higher dimensional awareness, but you will get really good at it in no time at all.

This entire process is natural as you continue to ascend, open and expand your conscious awareness. You ultimately ping pong back and forth until you light up to your entire energy system and stabilize the chakras. The more you surrender to this process and explore what is possible within you, the easier it is to calibrate your energy.

Trust yourself in this process!

INSULATE – PROTECTING YOUR ENERGY

Now that you have worked so hard to establish, cleanse and activate your energetic personal power, you want to learn how to protect it! Protecting your energy is an absolute necessity as a sensitive soul living in a world of duality.

Some worlds exist where only light exists, just like there are dimensions where there is only pure darkness. This is not one of them. We live in a world of both light and dark. In this realm, we perpetually learn about ourselves by moving closer or further from Source and our higher selves through interactions with both sides, the dark and the light.

The souls of empaths usually resonate with mostly light and are wired for a light existence. Living in a world of duality, unmanaged empaths tend to be energetically porous and super open to unseen influences where it's easy to absorb other people's energy and attract negative influences. This becomes incredibly confusing as it leads to frequency entanglement (discussed in Week 2).

"Is this my emotion or am I feeling the emotions of the person I'm with?" "Am I being influenced by this object I'm holding?" "Am I picking up on the energy from the environment that I'm in?" "Do I keep playing out fear that I absorbed from my parents long ago?"

Ignoring the need for energy protection opens yourself up to living in a darker world of fear and negativity that may not even originate from you! Fear and negativity ultimately prevents you from growing and keeps you easily controlled rather than the one easily in control.

The level of energy protection you need to practice depends on the level of fear in your daily life. A good way to gauge your general level of fear is to honestly evaluate where you are on the emotional scale on a regular basis.

Lower frequency emotions = more fear.

"Am I anxious to talk to my boss because I'm afraid I'll lose my job?" "Am I afraid to go on stage because I'm afraid people will judge me?" "Am I afraid to go after my dreams because I'm afraid I will fail?"

The more fear you carry, the more fear manifests. Fear begets more fear. The more fear you hold and carry within your energy, the more available you are to unseen influences like negative entities, who are attracted to the fear like bees are to flowers. They feed off of it. They love it when you are in fear because it means they get to feast off of your personal power leading you to become drained, lower your frequency and possibly become ill over time.

Negative entities can teach us a lot about ourselves in the sense that they show us where we may be energetically weaker or out of balance with our truth. They do serve a purpose but you don't have to live with them forever.

These darker entities, although very real, are purely opportunistic in nature. They need a way in to your energy in order to access you. I call these low vibe access points "potholes" or the soft spots within our aura. Whether it be a false belief you've carried since childhood, a fear based in the ego, or an emotional trigger due to a past traumatic situation, this is how they get in. If you don't clear your fear energy out and seal these potholes, it will keep your energy at a lower vibration so the negative influences can get in.

Are you familiar with the old wives tale that vampires cannot come into your home unless invited? Yeah, this is where that comes from. Don't invite them in!

The real truth that no one will tell you is that you truly have no need to be afraid of anything "unseen" because you always have the power, the choice, the sovereignty and ability to rise above and remove yourself from anything that does not serve you from a place of unconditional love. That is the absolute truth.

At the same time, that doesn't mean that negative entities don't exist, because they certainly do. And these entities are banking on the fact that you have forgotten how powerful you are and how capable you are of denying them access to your energy. Good thing you're reading this book to remind you that you can regain authority over yourself by protecting your energy! Yay you!

Step 1: Understanding Boundaries

We all have the right to personal boundaries. Whether you have been exercising your boundaries or not may be a different issue, but we all have the authority over ourselves to establish and enforce our own personal boundaries.

If you remember back to the energy vampires we were talking about in Week 2, there are individuals as well as institutions that depend on you not enforcing boundaries for yourself. They rely on the ability to easily manipulate or persuade you into doing their bidding. Knowing that these entities exist (in the physical and the spirit world) and considering how precious and tasty your energy is to them, it is your responsibility to protect yourself!

Boundaries are a widely used term but rarely do we understand the extent of how we can set boundaries for ourselves, or the extent to which our boundaries are being over stepped.

Physical Boundaries

Physical boundaries has to do with establishing consent for your physical body. If, when, how and where you would like to be touched or interacted with.

A general example of this boundary being ignored is someone who feels they can grab things out of your hand without asking or someone who stands too close while talking to you. These are both instances where your physical boundaries are not being considered.

There are varying degrees in which our physical boundaries need to be enforced. A nursing mother needs to make herself physically available for her child whenever they are hungry so she will have looser physical boundaries with her child. Whereas she may not be as physically accessible to her husband every time he is interested in being intimate with her, especially after a full day of childcare, so she may have different boundaries with him for the time being.

The same also goes for making yourself physically available to the public. If you work in an office building and your desk is near the front door, everyone who walks through that front door will have access to you and your attention. Whereas the person who has a private corner office with a closed door is physically inaccessible by comparison.

In extreme cases of physical boundaries, being hit, pushed, aggressively provoked or touched inappropriately is considered abusive. Physical and sexual abuse is never, ever, ever ok and if this is your current experience, please seek help immediately.

Where in your life do you need to enforce stronger physical boundaries?

_____

_____

_____

Time Boundaries

Time boundaries aren't just for billable hours anymore! In society, it has become such normal practice to give away our time so freely. Spending time on tasks that don't benefit you. Sharing your time with people who don't elevate you. Doing jobs that are purely production just for the sake of a paycheck.

Examples of this boundary not being honored includes a boss who makes you work late often without asking if it is ok with you. The kiosk at the mall asking you to stop and give a few moments of your time to hear their sales pitch for something you're really not interested in. The family member who ignores you when you say you have to leave or get off the phone and they just keep talking.

Again, there are varying degrees of how to implement boundaries on your time. Are you spending too much time cleaning up someone else's mess in the house when you could be using that time for meditation or self care? Or maybe there is a routine process in your life that can be simplified or expedited to cut down on the amount of time you spend on it, freeing up more time for creative activities or fun!

Your time is like an energy bank account. How can you spend it more wisely?

_____

_____

_____

_____

Financial Boundaries

Financial boundaries has to do with how, where and why you spend your money. How accessible is your money or spending potential to others? It also has to do with what you are willing to do for the sake of money.

An example of this boundary being overstepped is when you loan someone money and they never pay you back because you're family or they see you as financially better off than them. Or maybe you pay for someone's meal once and then they assume that you will always pay for meals going forward. It's one thing if you want to pay for all the meals out of enjoyment. It's a different energy once it is assumed and expected.

Financial boundaries are a common one for unmanaged empaths to struggle with. We can equate money to love all too often. I love you so much that I will spend money on you to match how much I love you — all the way until you are drowning in debt.

A healthy financial boundary is having an awareness and respect for the money that flows in and out of your life as well as appreciation for what it takes to attract that abundance into your bank account and acting accordingly.

Where in your life are you able to strengthen your financial boundaries?

_____

_____

_____

Energetic Boundaries

Energetic boundaries is one that is frequently overlooked since we often are not taught how to even be energetically aware in the first place. You can have your energy drained by all kinds of things: a person or group of people, a task, an activity, a situation, an environment, or even global location. Anything that is siphoning our energy without you even realizing it has a claim on your energy without your permission.

If you find that someone or something demands your focus or attention when you wouldn't offer it freely, this is an indication that your energetic boundaries need to be more strongly enforced.

An example of this boundary being encroached upon can be summarized by taking a quick drive down the main shopping strip in your home town. You may notice a long line of neon signs, stores advertising sales, bright colors and lights trying to get your attention, maybe even a sign-spinner or two in an attempt to get you to pull in and get your business. These are all attempts to get your attention when driving safely is the real priority that deserves your attention the most.

This boundary is often impeded on in the sneakiest of ways because so much is cleverly designed to be subliminal energy drains. Think for a moment about the addictive nature of social media, apps or video games. These constantly request our attention with notifications, bells, alarms, deadlines and alerts. It is designed to draw you in and absorb your attention for as long and as often as possible. You do not have full control over your focus when you're sucked into something designed to retain it.

Something as simple as not changing the battery in your smoke detector and allowing it to beep is a drain on your focus, ultimately weakening your personal power.

Take a look at your surroundings right now. What is within your vicinity that demands your attention and could be a drain on your energetic boundaries?

_____

_____

_____

Step 2: The Lesson of Setting Boundaries

Boundaries are a big deal which is why we are spending an entire week on them. But why are boundaries so important?

Imagine now having a private moment on a picnic blanket in a park with your partner. Imagine the conversation is quite heated and of a personal nature where emotions are running high. How would it feel if someone comes over, steps all over your blanket, knocks over your food and interrupts your intense conversation just to pet your dog without asking permission. In fact, they don't even acknowledge you. They don't look at you or talk to you, but rather fully engage in conversation of baby talk with your dog. Are you going to feel open and receptive with this person if they needed a favor? Or would you feel guarded and maybe even a little ticked off at their complete disregard for you and what you were doing?

Dishonoring or disrespecting boundaries is the social equivalent to a male boss just staring at the breasts of a female employee when talking to her. Not only is this a major social faux pas, but a clear violation of the person feeling safe enough to be open. It serves as an indicator that the dominating energy does not acknowledge nor respect the other person's boundaries or comfort level.

Domineering or over-bearing energy immediately creates an unbalanced energy dynamic. One person is asserting control over the situation or the other person. It completely takes the power away from the person in the submissive role.

By allowing boundaries to be disregarded or allowing something like the above examples to continue without saying anything, it won't feel good. Why? By remaining silent or permitting the dominance to occur, you are essentially agreeing to disempowerment. How powerful can you possibly feel when in a minimized or diminished state of energy?

This unbalanced power dynamic doesn't just occur with strangers in the park or bosses staring down your shirt. It plays out in our closest relationships. Just because you are fabulously intuitive and reading this book for some incredible self development, doesn't mean you're in the clear. This goes both ways. Just because you've had your boundaries ingratiated upon doesn't mean that you are the only victim here. You have more responsibility here than you may realize.

Start to pay attention to where do you get YOUR energy from. Do you feel recharged after hanging out with that one friend who always listens to you dump your emotional garbage? Do you only call her when things are going wrong in your life? What feeling do you leave her with after each conversation?

If you don't have a firm sense of enforcing your own boundaries, you can bet money that you are overstepping other people's boundaries and not even realizing it. The fact of the matter is you can't honor anyone else's boundaries until you prioritize your own and you will see this play out time and time again.

The State of 'No' and the State of 'Yes'

Sometimes you may go a little overboard in an attempt to protect your energy and completely shut down everything. All of your energy goes into lock down mode in an attempt to maintain boundaries when you don't know how to discern or maintain your power in various situations. Energetically speaking, this will put you into what I call "the state of no" where you are closed off to absolutely everything: incoming love, kind gestures, new information, new opportunities, witnessing the magic of life, you will miss all of it.

Now sometimes being in the state of 'no' is beneficial because you may be in a deep healing process where you need to conserve all of your energy while you restore and recover yourself from whatever you have been through. When struggling with feelings of overwhelm or an inability to deal with current circumstances, closing off your energetic receptivity allows you to focus all your energy on mending and strengthening yourself. However long you need to remain in a closed-off state while you recover is up to you and what you need. Just know at some point, you will need to open up your energy once again in order to grow.

The state of 'yes' is what allows you to begin receiving new energy! New ideas! New possibilities! New offers! New information! New helpful people! New relationships! New psychic downloads! It's all possible in the state of yes because you're open to it!

Shifting from a state of 'no' into a more receptive space of 'yes' enables you to open your heart energy, welcome in new information and opportunities, and allow in anything that may not have been considered before because you didn't have the space for it then.

To shift from the state of 'no' into the state of 'yes' relies upon a heavy faith that all is unfolding and working out in your favor — because it is! Even if it doesn't seem to be going the way which you would like it to, trusting that the Universe and your angels always have your best interest at heart is what will support the transition from a 'no' to a 'yes'.

Step 3: Energetic Protection

Insulating your energy through awareness and protection needs to be your go-to as you navigate this world with eyes wide open. You are your own best advocate. It is literally no one else's job in the entire universe to make sure your boundaries are respected — except for you.

If you are feeling as if your boundaries are being overstepped or you're not sure why you are feeling uncomfortable in a certain situation, take yourself through the following steps to know where, how and with whom you need to set a boundary.

1. **Awareness:** the first step is simply being aware that your energy is being encroached upon. You can ask yourself, what is being affected here? My time? My money? My energy? Get clear on how you are being intruded upon.

2. **Identify:** You now have a choice to make. Do you express your boundary to the offending party or do you suppress your truth due to emotional triggers, old programming or fear?

3. **Decide:** Make the choice. This has the potential of being a very liberating moment for you, if you choose wisely. Express your truth by declaring your boundary rather than suppressing your truth and letting it fester. This will only turn into resentment later on.

4. **Maintain:** Hold your position no matter the reaction. Stay strong in the ability to speak your truth and allow the other person to have their reactions. If setting boundaries is a new thing for you, people won't expect it. Sometimes they may not like it. Know that this is a reflection of them, not you, and continue to stay true to YOU.

Maintaining your boundaries also applies to when you are developing yourself psychically. When exploring other realms and dimensions, boundaries are just as important!

For example, when setting the intention to create a sacred healing space to do energy work, it is imperative that you are strong enough to maintain your own energetic boundary. When you are strong in yourself, nothing malevolent gets in. The converse is also true. If you set the intention that you are safe enough to tune into and work with your outer chakras but you also fear that something will attach to you while you're meditating, that fear is exactly what leaves your energetic boundary open and at risk.

The 3D world that we live in is like the playing field to practice owning your true power. So when you get into exploring the cosmos and you bump into a being that doesn't have your best interest at heart (happens more often than you'd think for some), you are strong enough to enforce your boundaries. Know that you are strong, therefore know that you are safe.

Step 4: Exercises for Insulation

Phone a Friend

Call in for help! You've got the direct line to Source so you can call in protection at anytime you need. Reach into your heart and ask for reinforcements that you know and trust. Call in God, command the light, summon your angels, guardian angels, guardian beings or protection spirits. Call in your dragon if that feels good for you. Call them in to create a barrier to assist you until you feel strong enough to hold your own boundaries. Also calling in higher frequencies can positively impact your own vibration if you've been vibrating lower in a state of fear.

Bubbling

Bubbling, also known as shielding, places you in an energetic container of protection. You can set the intention to place yourself in an energetic bubble by visualizing an energy orb around you. If visualizing isn't your strongest suit yet, simply feel or speak an intention of protection. You can imagine (quite literally) what you would look like in a bubble of light. You can fill it with a blue gel that slows down any energy that doesn't belong to you, preventing it from reaching you. You can even imagine throwing a little glitter in that bubble with you just for fun and extra light!

A **mirrored ball** is another option. Imagine you are placed within a mirrored ball so energy or unwanted attention that is coming towards you is reflecting off of your energy.

You can even affirm your mirrored ball by saying out loud "Let others see what they need to see so that I am free to be me. So it is."

Shielding is also a fun exercise to practice when protecting your energy. If you are feeling someone else's pain or emotional intensity and it's just too much, you can shield your heart from absorbing it. Imagine a shield coming out from the heart space to deflect anything sharp energy coming towards you.

You can even use this shield over your gut if someone or something is attempting to pull on your personal power. When you feel the energy pulling at you, throw up a shield to deflect that energy. It's not yours to absorb.

Set Boundaries

This can be challenging for many unmanaged empaths initially because there may be wounds that convince you that you need to keep your boundaries low or non-existent for various reasons.

You may rationalize not setting boundaries for yourself, like *"if I don't answer this call, this person will think I don't love them."* Catch yourself if you're doing this and use this as an opportunity to set solid boundaries for yourself. We have covered enough about boundaries to know this will result in you being too depleted. By saying yes or being available to too many things, ultimately very draining.

A simple example of setting a boundary on your time, you could say *"I only have 15 minutes to talk."* An example of a financial boundary might be an agreement that we are only to spend $100 on birthday gifts this year. And whatever you declare for a boundary, honor your own energy by honoring your word. Don't go back on it.

Remove Your Energy

You have the freedom to remove yourself or leave any situation that is not good for you. When you have already set boundaries for yourself by speaking your truth and you are still not being heard, other options may not be enough. This option not only gets your point across but it ultimately protects you.

This is good for toxic or draining situations like a group chat that is distracting during family time or an unequal relationship where you're doing all the emotional investing, or a job that doesn't pay you what you're worth.

As you raise your vibration, you will notice more and more what doesn't line up with your worth. You gain clarity on just how valuable you are and what matches or doesn't match what you have to offer. When you're spending more energy than you're receiving, its a disservice to everyone involved. Put the figurative oxygen mask on yourself first and remove yourself from the unhealthy situation. Your energy is a gift with whomever you choose to share it with, don't ever forget that.

Anchor Cords

Using anchor cords to connect to the Earth's core can establish energetic protection. It is similar to grounding in the sense that you set an intention, or visualize a tap root coming out from your root chakra and plugging into the iron core of the Earth.

When there is a lot going on in your environment like a lot of other people present, a lot of chatter, a lot of movement and stimulation, we can feel totally overwhelmed and get swept up in the overstimulation. Use anchor cording to plug yourself into the crystalline grid and draw up earth energy. That energy is pure, solid energy that anchors and stabilizes you, making it easier to discern what to pay attention to and what to ignore while standing in your power.

Protection Ceremony or Spell

If you find that your energy keeps getting impeded upon over and over again but you're not able to remove yourself from the situation, this is a helpful option. If there is someone in your life who continues to overstep boundaries or you're having trouble discerning where your boundaries need to be with someone, invoking your higher power through ceremonial intention may be supportive for your situation.

This is appropriate in examples such as you have a responsibility to an elderly family member who is particularly needy but they are not respectful or aware of your boundaries, ceremony work may help moving forward in this situation. Or let's say you have a boss who operates in a codependent manner but you're not ready or able to leave your job quite yet, a protection ceremony can call in the big guns to help keep your energy safe as you navigate this life circumstance.

As far as what ceremony or ritual to perform, this is a very personal choice. Whatever feels good to you and does no harm unto others, do that.

Protection Crystals

There is a crystal out there for literally any intention you may have, so why not work with them to enhance your energetic protection?

Crystals such as black tourmaline, onyx, obsidian, labradorite, angel phantom quartz, shungite, carbon quartz, Apache tears, Staurolite "fairy cross stone" or flourite are great options for fortifying your aura and reinforcing your energetic boundaries and intentions. Wear them, carry them, sleep with them, keep them in your purse, your car or get fancy and try crystal gridding your home. This will serve you well.

Close Energy Circuit and Clear

Sometimes we can unconsciously shrink ourselves to accommodate imposing energies trying to move into our domain. Momentarily closing your energy off to outside sources allows you to protect your energy and clear whatever needs to be cleared to reclaim your space.

This practice is like entering into a state of 'no' but only for the moment. Lay your hands over one another (in no particular order) and place them over the solar plexus chakra. Imagine, visualize or intend that you are flushing your entire system with white light from Source to release any energy that is not yours.

Next visualize you are pushing your energy field back out to reclaim your space that has been invaded.

And so it is.

Community of Trust

This exercise is for the long game. Only allow people into your life (and to stay in your life) that honor and respect your energy as well as your boundaries.

If you have a friend who is constantly draining you because they choose to live their life in chaos and you are always the one who sympathizes with them, maybe it's time to re-evaluate if that friendship is genuinely serving you.

Sometimes making the right choice is the most difficult choice — but it's the choice that will ultimately protect your energy reserves and serve your highest good.

WEEK 7

INTEGRATE –
TYPES OF EMPATHS

By learning more about being an empath in general, you are able to identify sensitive areas that may have once been seen as a weakness or vulnerability. You may now begin to see them as a part of your super powers!

If you're not feeling super powerful just yet, fear not. We will now explore the different types of empath there are which will help you to fully integrate the various aspects of your innate strengths, empowering you as an empath overall!

Empaths are natural-born "feelers". You feel so much by having a higher degree of sensory awareness, as well as maintaining the ability to merge with a separate energetic reality of someone or something outside of yourself.

There are many different ways an individual empath can connect with the energy or consciousness of another and many different types of relationships an empath may form naturally.

There is no hard and fast rule for types of empaths. The following types listed simply refer to a set of dominant strengths, skills and preferences for spiritual gifts I've observed in myself and others during my work with sensitive souls over the years (and lifetimes). Please know these can evolve over time and often do. Most likely, your soul has spent a lifetime or two or three or five hundred mastering the inherent skills you come into this life with. These skills and abilities may be evident fairly early on in life or may lie dormant for many years, awaiting a spontaneous awakening to unearth these natural talents.

Also, you are most probably more than one type of empath; meaning, you have the ability to connect to more than one type of being in more than one way. It's not only possible, but it's actually common to have more than one type of empathy ability. Most often these various empathic skillsets are used collaboratively to develop a unique soul calling or role for you to play here on earth.

Whether you connect with humans more so than plants, or healing crystals and stones over animals, these are all different types of empathy. Discovering the type of empath you are is an important step in determining how you can best use your gifts, and therefore develop them further.

For example, you are a natural animal empath and have always had a knack for knowing about and caring for animals. If you were to take a peak into your Akashic Records (the records of all-that-is and all there ever was), you may see that you spent lifetimes as a sheep hearder, farmer, animal caretaker and maybe even living as the animals themselves!

Figuring out which type(s) of empath you are can also additionally help with the age-old question of "what is my purpose?" Empathy is closely linked to the soul gifts that we are born with. Illuminating these gifts help guide us to the work that we most aligned with doing during our time here on Earth.

Which of the following empath types do you relate to?

Step 1: Identify Your Type(s)

Emotional Empath

The most commonly understood type of empath is the emotional empath. This empath can feel, experience and absorb the emotions of others.

Strengths
Emotional empaths make great friends, partners, spouses, parents, counselors, midwives, teachers, marketing representatives, guides, therapists, performers, motivational speakers, working with an audiences and crisis hotline responders as their gifts help with understanding the emotional needs of people, even when others don't understand their own emotional needs.

Challenges
It can be quite confusing and overwhelming when you are feeling so many emotions that do not originate with you. You may feel as though you are overly emotional, have bipolar tendencies, easily depressed, wild mood swings, easily anxious, moody, or even feel unpredictable. These emotions can stay with you and influence the rest of your day, or even

your life, if you don't identify these emotions have been absorbed and clear them.

Example
You're standing in line at the grocery store. You had a great day. Suddenly you notice the flustered woman in front of you being nasty to the checkout clerk. You feel quite anxious, maybe even suddenly irritated that the check out person is taking so long. You feel anxious that this isn't moving along quicker. You have just absorbed the emotional state of the woman in front of you in line. This may not even become clear until she leaves and you feel it lessening within you as you leave the store.

How to Develop
If you're interested in developing your emotional empathy, begin by getting clear on your own emotional baseline. Get confident with grounding and clearing your energy, as well as strengthening your boundary-setting abilities.

From there, you may experiment with stepping more fully into your senses. Take the time to get out of your head. Stop trying to analyze what something means or the reason behind things and just allow yourself to feel what you are feeling while remaining unattached and neutral. Observe emotions as they come up. Identify whether what you are feeling belongs to you or does it come from someone or somewhere else? Have you been influenced to feel this way? Does this emotion feel true to your heart?

You may even want to explore these feelings further by journaling about them or speaking them aloud. You don't even need to say it to someone else but just simply declaring something out loud to yourself. See how it feels when you say it. Does the energy feel strong, like it is your truth? Or does the energy feel weak when you say it, like maybe you are just parroting something you absorbed from someone else?

Intellectual Empath

Intellectual empaths are extremely perceptive in the sense that they naturally understand how people think. Thought processes can vary from person to person; how they come to conclusions, how linear or non-linear their thinking is, what reaction will result or even understanding the path on how they go from point A to point B in their learning processes. Due the the wide variety in an individuals background, cultural conditioning, education and even health status, all of these things can factor into how a person thinks. Intellectual empaths don't need to know the details of a person's life or personality in order to understand and clearly see the way the an individual or group may think.

Strengths
Intellectual empaths naturally understand people's motives or thought process behind their words and actions. This is great for conflict resolution and problem solving, knowing what information to accept and what to dismiss because you are able to see where the information or communication is coming from. Intellectual empaths are not easily fooled or manipulated because you can see right through deception and persuasion. You can also excel in work or projects where something needs to be tailored to a certain group such as in user interface work or educational curriculum.

Challenges

An unmanaged intellectual empath can struggle with being too mentally focused, stuck in analyzing state or even feel you are better than everyone else because you are mentally faster than most. If you have not done the work on opening the heart chakra, you may lack emotional empathy. You may become too narrowly focused missing sentiment or sincerity due to the need to understand how did they come to that conclusion? This may evolve into a lack of trust. It's also possible to lose yourself if too much time is spent trying to think like others, rather than honoring your own organic process. An ego-centric intellectual empath may even use your gifts to try to change other people's minds or get what you want from people.

Example

Different people have different thought processes in order to arrive at a conclusion or result. As an intellectual empath, you may have a much faster processing speed than those you are connecting with. For example, if you can remember back to the days of grade school, getting bored in class, having to pay attention to the teacher explaining something starting at point A, to point B, to point C, all the way to point Z. She does this to ensure every student comprehends the lesson.

Whereas, you may not need that laborious drawn-out process. You may have already gone from point A to point Z, then jumped back to point D, then M, then thought about what you want for lunch, then maybe what you will do after school later, then the birds outside may get your attention and then you might have a conversation with them in your mind, then you might tune back in to what the teacher is saying and she is only at point

M, so you tune back out all the while the rest of the class is slow to keep up.

How to Develop
As an intellectual empath, it is important to cultivate the heart charka and stay in tune with what your heart is saying at all times. As you stay connected to your heart, be patient with others who may not mentally process things as quickly as you do. Otherwise you can get lost in your mental processes and become out of reach to those around you.

Your gift of intellectual acuity is a gift that is meant to be shared. One way to develop this gift is to do volunteer work within communities in need. As an example, working with those who are developmentally disabled will allow you to tune into someone who operates very differently from most. You may be able to pick up on needs or tendencies that may be missed otherwise and by your presence and observation, you have the opportunity to positively impact their life completely!

Physical Empath

Physical empaths, can also be known as Medical empaths, absorb the physical state of another person. These empaths are able to understand information and connect to the health of another, even without medical training.

This can manifest in a number of ways depending on the strongest senses of the empath. The physical empath may physically feel someone else's pain as if it is your own. You may be able to see someone's illness in their mind's eye. You may be able to predict an injury or illness, or sense a past injury that hasn't fully healed. You may hear a person's body or organ asking for help, such as a vitamin deficiency or oncoming seizure.

Strengths

Physical empaths make incredible medical intuitives, somatic body workers, physical therapists, energy healers, naturopaths, pediatricians, nursing home attendants and shamans. You are also excellent at helping those who can't communicate their needs such as one who is in a coma, suffering from locked-in syndrome, or simply speaks another language and cannot communicate the issue at hand. Alternatively, physical empaths can also assist detectives in cold cases by connecting with the consciousness of the victim and replaying what they went through physically.

Challenges

Physical empaths have a unique challenge as you may attach and identify to someone else's physical symptoms as your own. You may develop a "mystery illness" where doctors cannot pinpoint the reasons for your presenting symptoms. This can also occur with "hereditary" illnesses, where you are actually absorbing other people's physical symptoms through acceptance of belief rather than legitimate illness. If skin issues or cancer runs in your family, be careful this is not a self-fulfilling prophecy where you are just absorbing and carrying the energy just to recreate it.

Example

An unmanaged empath will have great difficulty visiting a nursing home or a hospital due to the overwhelming absorbing or so many physical maladies. You may feel physically ill when inside the building yet feel relief once you leave.

How to Develop
If you're interested in developing your gifts of physical empathy, it is imperative that you get yourself feeling in top notch health first!

Give up any habit that is currently polluting your body. Ditch the soda and quit the sugar. Eliminate processed foods and stay away from anything that lists "natural flavor" as an ingredient. You may explore detoxing your body through various methods such as a juice cleanse, eating only clean, whole foods, doing intermittent fasting or trying a 24 hour water fast.

By clearing your body of toxins, you are clearing your channel to allow energy to flow. You are also establishing health and wellness as a baseline. So whenever you feel like anything is off, you can register this feeling as energetic information due to your skills of physical empathy and not default to a fear-based thought of *"oh no, am I sick?"*

Sexual Empath

Sexual empaths can administer healing activations, energy clearings, therapeutic releases through sexual energy, expression and interaction. You have an understanding of (and may identify with) many or all possibilities on the sexual spectrum.

Strengths
Sexual empaths assist those with twisted energies stuck in the sacral centers by embodying healing energies and unconditional love during

intimate practices and exchange. This allows wounded individuals to experience a higher form of sexual exchange to compare with imbalanced past experiences. Connecting with a sexual empath may catalyze a spiritual awakening for self or the partner through sexual acts and intimate exchange practices. Healing can take place within partnerships and energy can profoundly shift, alchemize and transform. Relationships can deepen, bodies can heal and strengthen, and dreams can be made manifest through this work.

Sexual intercourse does not always need to be present in order for a sexual empath to transmit your healing effects. Sexual empaths may become energy healers, massage therapists, tantra teachers, yoga instructors, couples counselors, spiritual teachers and healing channels.

Challenges
An unmanaged sexual empath may struggle with many experiences where you are taken advantage of sexually, or may even experience severe sexual trauma. You may spend long periods of time being sexually confused, traumatized or even celibate due to the challenges that result from absorbing other people's sexual energy. The presence of a sexual empath often causes the buried sexual trauma of others to surface during or after sexual exchange. You then may absorb and take on the trauma or victimization of the partner's sexual issues. Sexual empaths may find themselves in unsatisfying relationships as you unknowingly are drawn to heal others but do not receive the same sacred intimacy in return.

Example
You have been in a relationship or situation with someone who has severe trauma. There are issues in their life that they have

not dealt with yet. Historically, they have not been able to meet you equally in an unconditionally loving partnership, yet they come in and out of your life any time they are going through a hard time. They are essentially getting a fix off of your love.

After falling into bed together, you believe things will be different this time because they seem different after being with you, yet over time the pattern repeats. What is occurring here? This person is doing something known as "spiritual bypassing." They are avoiding doing their own spiritual work, refusing to look at themselves and their own issues to fix their life. They are instead using you and your sexual healing abilities to transmute their own painful or difficult energy, which you ultimately absorb and are left to deal with.

How to Develop
In order to develop your abilities as a sexual empath, you must first heal any sexual trauma within yourself. Balance and clear your sacral energies, remove any influences that are harmful to your sexual energy such as pornography or toxic sexual relationships. Establish solid boundaries in all of your relationships and develop self love before exchanging sexual energies with anyone else.

Doing this work will take time. This world that we are in has literally built billion-dollar industries that prey upon the purity of sexual creation energy and disturbs healthy development by gaining access to your purity without you knowing. Please be patient with yourself as you move through this process. This stuff goes really deep.

When you feel open and ready, explore the healing arts of tantra, sensual communication and true intimacy practices with a trusted partner who honors and respects you. Learn more about sex magic and how your sexual energy holds a power that can be used towards manifestation and creation. Play with running your sexual energy through various chakras and observe the experience.

Plant Empath

Plant empaths have the innate ability to join consciousness with plant life, trees, plants, flowers, grass, and even fungi. By gaining access to higher chakras where higher frequencies are able to register, plant empaths are essentially able to commune with Mother Gaia and the living network of beings that make up her biosystem, creating a symbiotic relationships of nourishment, healing and caution where necessary.

Strengths
Plant empaths work really well with using plants for their many practical applications and purposes. Plants can be used as medicine, nutrition, air detoxifiers, environmental clean up, plant spirit work, health care, beauty, essential oils, healing herbs, fuel sources, building supplies and cleaning agents to name a few. Plant empaths are able to easily ground and energetically regenerate by being in Nature.

Challenges
Plant empaths have unique challenges due to the deep connection felt with the plant life on the planet. It can be difficult to see a yard unkept or a dying houseplant in someone's home. It can be downright traumatizing to witness deforestation or widespread disregard for the environment. Plant empaths tend

to be a very sensitive breed as you are so finely tuned to "listen" to the plants speak. Drug addiction is a common struggle for many plant empaths at some point in your lifetime. Ironically, working with healing plants including cannabis can assist in tackling any serious addiction issue.

Example
When you go to a new doctor's office, the first thing you may notice is how happy the plants are in the waiting room, whereas others who first walk into the office may first notice the brightly colored curtains on the wall or the long waiting line. You then may prefer to take herbal remedies or naturopathic medicines over any pharmaceuticals the doctor may try to prescribe.

How to Develop
There are so many satisfying ways to develop gifts of plant empathy: starting your own indoor or outdoor garden, growing your own food, developing a relationship with your houseplants, working with tinctures or Bach flower remedies, drinking teas for nutritional benefits, dieting herbs to familiarize yourself with the plant spirit, working with plant medicine such as San Pedro or Ayahuasca with a trusted shaman or practitioner.

Crystal Empath

Crystal empaths, also referred to as mineral empaths, connect with the consciousness of crystals, rocks and gemstones. There is a reason that crystals, stones and gems are highly regarded around the planet and crystal empaths can sense many reasons why. Natural mineral formations carry a vibrational structure that carries it's own kind of intelligence. The frequencies emitted by crystals and natural minerals can be used in supportive and beneficial ways to humans as they can affect all bodies of consciousness. One crystal has the ability to work with a human within their causal body, spiritual body, mental body, emotional body and physical body in a number of ways. Crystal empaths are able to tap into this crystal technology and utilize it for its many advanced, and often underestimated, capabilities.

Strengths
Crystal empaths can use crystal healing energy to change, heal and transform areas of your life and others' lives utilizing crystal frequencies. By intuitively knowing which crystal to work with (maybe without really knowing why you are drawn to a crystal) and knowing where on the body to place the crystal, healing codes can be activated and exchanged within the bodies of consciousness. Crystal empaths often have comfortable homes with warm and soothing energy due to the many crystals placed round the home. You also make excellent crystal and energy healers, jewelers, geologists, chemists, rock hounds, collectors, designers

Challenges
Addiction to buying, collecting and hoarding rocks and crystals, afraid to share or give away gemstone, rocks or crystals.

Example
You are naturally drawn to the beauty and intricacy of crystals and stones. As a kid, you couldn't go out to play without coming home with your pockets full of stones.

How to Develop

Crystals are an enhancement to your life. Whether you are in a place of grief and deep healing or in a place of prosperous growth and creation, crystals can and will help you! They are not biased and are very easy to work with. Crystals will let you know when you might need to connect with them by drawing in your curiosity. They may seem especially beautiful or appealing to you or they may come into your life as a gift or spontaneous find. They will also let you know when your work is done by disappearing for a while or you may have an aversion to certain ones. Listen to this inner guidance as you will feel pulled or repelled by the crystal energies that compliment you.

Another option to develop your crystal healing abilities is to take a course or read a book on working with crystals. I have an entire book that walks you through all the ins and outs of working with crystals, including practice exercises and recipes for making crystal elixirs.

Crystal healing was my first love on my spiritual journey and I just couldn't get enough of these beautiful high-frequency friends. I still practice crystal healing daily as it truly becomes a part of your life when you're a crystal empath.

Reading List!

If you'd like more information on working with the healing power of crystals such as crystal gridding, making crystal elixirs and balancing chakras using stone work, here is my book to check out:

1. Crystal Healing Work: A Complete Course, Kate Moriah Kyser.

Animal Empath

Animal empaths easily relate to animals, as they can communicate and exchange information with animals that are living or have crossed over. Animal empaths may love communicating with animals as a whole or they may feel drawn to specific animals or animal categories, such as birds or aquatic mammals.

Karl von Frisch was an intuitive ethologist who won the Nobel prize for noticing that honey bees communicate the direct location of food sources to the rest of the hive. By observing the honey bees waggle dance, von Frisch was able to interpret the meaning of the bee's moves in relation to the information being communicated to its fellow bees. Only an animal empath would be able to tune into that!

Strengths
Animal empaths have a knack for understanding, and even being amused by the various personalities, information and feedback given by an animal, either living or departed. They are able to communicate on a totally different level than humans interact as it is a very heart-based method of communication, so connecting outside of the physical realm is not an issue. Animal empaths can assist in situations where an animal may be lost, wounded, in distress, in need of medical care, has an ongoing issue that has not been easily resolved or is ready to pass on.

Animal empaths make excellent animal communicators, animal healers, veterinarians, vet techs, farmers, farm vets, sanctuary workers, animal foster parents, advocates, artists, humorists, content creators, and rescuers to name a few.

Challenges

Animal empaths can experience a lot of challenges in this world because this world is not very kind to our animal friends. The mistreatment of animals in the food and clothing industry, as well as irresponsible or careless animal owners, can easily trigger an animal empath to experience the animal's pain as if your own. You can be severely affected by visions of hurt animals or any kind of abuse. This also tends to affect your diet and what you can eat as you may struggle with whether to eat animal protein and animal products or not. There is no right or wrong answer, as it is a personal choice.

Example

You are invited to a friend's house for a birthday party. Rather than spending time with the people at the party, you find you're spending all your time with the cat or the dog that lives there. You prefer to hang out with them the whole time because they are more fun than interacting with humans and make better company in your opinion. By the time you leave the party, you find the animal to be the most memorable part of the evening.

How to Develop

Developing animal empathy may be something that you find just comes naturally. Animal empaths naturally gravitate towards interacting with animals. The more time you spend with animals, the better as familiarizing yourself with animals elevates your connection. Being present, observing the details, listening with all of your senses — these are keys to effective animal communication.

If you don't already have any animals in your home, you may want to keep an animal and care for it. You may consider adopting a sick or older animal and working with them to administer healing, like Reiki energy or just living in a stable home environment to live out their days in peace.

Explore options such as guided meditations. I have a video on my blog specifically walking you through an exercise for animal communication called *A Guided Exercise on How to Communicate with Animals*. (https://projectempath.com/blogs/recent/a-guided-exercise-on-how-to-communicate-with-animals)

You may even call in a spirit animal to be a guide to assist you in your efforts to communicate with animals. Work with this animal spirit over time to learn more about how animals communicate.

Before you know it, you'll be having full conversations and exchanging jokes with the neighbor's dog!

Environmental Empath

An environmental empath, also referred to as a location empath, connects to the energetic consciousness of the surrounding environment or a specified physical location. By tuning into and communicating with the energy of a land or area, information can be derived, such as historical events, potentially missed opportunities within the space (as seen with water divination) or even discovering when a land healing is needed.

Strengths
Environmental empaths can tap into and learn from the energetic information that has been imprinted on a location. Using intuition,

these empaths can find historical inaccuracies, assist in spacial clearings and promote feng shui flow through out environments. Environmental empaths can also develop into doing energy space clearings, land blessings, or even remote viewing. These powerful empaths can identify what needs to be done to heal, restore or regenerate a land area, such as a reforestation project or bringing in new plants to assist the current ecosystem. Water diviners, although a dying breed in most parts, are also a great example of an environmental empath.

Challenges
Unmanaged environmental empaths can get sick from being in a negative environment as you are severely affected by the energy of others. This can also include old energy like negative energy loops that were created long ago. Visiting historical sites or places that has seen tragedy like a battle ground can feel uncomfortable or even make the empath physically ill.

Environmental empaths can feel unhealthily attachment to or overly protective of a place or land that they may not have physical or legal rights to. This may be difficult as they may not have a say in decisions that are made affecting the land.

You may be energetically blocked or feel lost in life if you are living in an area that does not energetically and vibrationally support you on the earth grid. A physical move may need to happen to feel more in tune with your environment and aligned with your surroundings.

Example
You move into a new house and cannot find peace or get a good night's sleep. You are experiencing discomfort, noises

in the home, restlessness, weird dreams, or having things disappear or move around your home without you moving them. Others may believe the house is haunted but you feel intuitively that the land is unhappy. You then discover that the property was once a slaughterhouse and there is an unmarked animal bone burial ground nearby and the spirits have been restless. They are not at peace. You understand this is why you are experiencing the same restless, agitated energy in your home. You connect to the land, honor those who have been forgotten, ask the traumatized energy to clear from the soil, mark the burial site with offerings of crystals and flowers, and contact a historical society to record your findings. The troubled energy has been put to rest.

How to Develop

Environmental empaths need to spend loads of time outdoors, taking in your surroundings and remaining undisturbed long enough to really commune with your environment without interruption. A place with a lot of stimulation, activity or competing energies will feel like too much for an environmental empath to listen clearly.

You may be interested in learning about the history of places, traveling to experience various energies, or studying maps to absorb the layout of the land.

Engaging in ritual and communing with your local environment will also enhance your ability to communicate with the land. Make offerings to the land, connect with the elemental guardians of the area, such as fairies, gnomes, and tree spirits, introduce yourself as a friend and admirer of their role and work. Befriend the energy. It will be more than happy to engage in communication when you display reverence and respect for the other beings existing in the area.

Geosentient Empath

Geosentient empaths connect to the consciousness of planet earth and are deeply in tune with the Crystalline grid. You are prone to live resonant with the rhythms of mother nature and are often greatly affected by energy disturbances on the planet. Needless to say there are quite a few disturbances on the planet right now, so this is a tricky time for Geosentient empaths to navigate your own stability.

Strengths
Geosentient empaths can sense impending natural events and disasters, such as earth quakes, tsunamis and volcanic eruptions. You also know what areas would provide the most safety and access to resources when needed. You know how to communicate with the earth for ultimate harmony of human/land interaction.

Geosentient empaths are gifted in identifying the needs of an environment or understanding the healing necessary to restore balance of the Earth grid. This may include planting crystals, reorganizing an area by moving earth as intuitively directed, or building spiritual structures or healing temples in gateway points on the earth grid.

Geosentient empaths make fantastic horticulturists, community planners, landscape designers, florists, advocates, earth stewards, environmental scientists, geophysicists, storm chasers, meteorologists, homesteaders and more.

Challenges

Geosentient empaths are physically affected by the devastation on Earth such as forest fires, earthquakes, and even civil unrest. You may feel emotional in areas where the land has absorbed trauma such a war, biological devastation or satanic rituals.

Example

You naturally gravitate towards learning about the native flora and fauna to the area that you're living. You feel more connected to your environment when you know more about it and how to care for it. You are motivated to learn more about how to thrive in harmony with all that earth has to offer. You take interest in how to work with your land to create a biorhythmic system so you can live harmoniously and continue to thrive. Systems that positively affect the multiple biodiverse systems within itself are of great value to you. An example such as collecting rain water to fill your outdoor fish pond, which then waters your garden and feeds your family.

How to Develop

To develop your geosentient empathic skills, develop your connection to mother earth. Live as in-tune with nature as you possibly can. Familiarize yourself with your local biodiversity, the climate, growing seasons, weather patterns, animal life, and ecological landscape. Eat and shop locally and organically. Ground yourself in mother earth's energy regularly. Honor the natural rhythms of your body, such as biological and circadian. Incorporate the bounty of nature's offerings into your daily life. Make this not only a practice, but a lifestyle choice.

Planetary Empath

Planetary empaths connect to the consciousness of planetary bodies. By attuning your focus to the cosmos, much practical information can be grounded and implemented when navigating life on earth. There is an inherent understanding that our life on this planet is greatly affected by our interconnectedness to our neighboring planetary bodies as well as our position in the universe.

Strengths
Planetary empaths understand energies, positions, aspects, and movements of planetary bodies in relation to humans and Earth. You make great astrologers, philosophers, astronomers, astrophysicists, quantum theorists, and teachers.

Challenges
Challenges that present for planetary empaths can relate to the position of certain planets and their affect on the natal chart. Depending on the span of time a difficult planetary aspect takes place, this can impede your day or your entire life.

Additional challenges may relate to past life memories or inherent knowledge of planetary realities that are not well-known to humanity, such as the existence of planets that have either been destroyed or hidden from humanity by controlling powers interested in concealing galactic histories and truth.

Example
You are fascinated with outerspace and find yourself having memories of being on a different planet at some stage within your soul's journey. Through past life regression, you are able to uncover lifetimes where you have existed on another planet. You

have very clear memories that are very different from what you have learned about the Universe from books on earth. You trust what you know more than what you have been taught to believe.

How to Develop
Dig into astrology or astronomy! Start paying attention to the planetary energies and how they affect life on earth.

Do meditations and listen to the songs of the planets. You can also choose to astral project to different planets. You can do this via shamanic journeying, working with psychedelics or entering into a hypnagogic trance. Visit with the energy, absorb the atmospheric frequencies, connect with the personality of the planet. When you come back, journal about your experience and what you witnessed or felt. You can tap into this energy for future spiritual explorative work and develop a relationship with the planet's consciousness.

Medium Empath

Medium empaths, usually referred to simply as a medium, are able to connect and communicate with souls that have departed from the physical earth plane, as well as earthbound spirits. Any human form of consciousness that has left physical form is able to be spoken to and heard from by a Medium empath. The messages are not always clear due to the various states a soul can be in, however, a medium empath is able to pick up any resonant energy around the person.

Strengths
Medium empaths can transmit healing messages to family and loved ones that may be grieving or stuck in a trauma loop

from the feelings of losing a loved one. Medium empaths have a deep understanding that death is an illusion and our spirit never truly dies, giving mediums a relative fearlessness when it comes to matters beyond the veil. Medium empaths can also support the solving of mysteries, correcting inaccurate history, finding lost objects and seeking justice for victims that can no longer seek it themselves. Mediums have the abilities to be a voice for the departed which is an incredible healing gift and profound responsibility.

Challenges

Seeing "ghosts" as a child and not being believed easily is a common struggle for medium empaths. Having the ability to see and hear voices from another world is not something that has been accepted as commonplace in most children. Historically this was considered normal. Yet by today's standards, it's only been in the most recent decade that we are hearing more and more about psychic children who speak with and see the dead.

Another challenge for medium empaths is often trickster energies and negative beings will impersonate a deceased loved one to be granted access to an unmanaged empaths energy. The empath will believe they are communicating with a dead loved one or a friendly spirit when really it is an advantageous energy vampire or demon lowering their vibration and fooling them with inaccurate information. This is a challenge that never truly disappears, though empowered medium empath learn and enforce boundaries, protection and discernment.

Example

You are staying at your grandmother's house for a week long visit. All week long, you keep having urges to go up to the attic.

You don't know why you would go up there. It's creepy, there's nothing important up there and no one has been up there for years, so you brush it off as nothing. Yet by the end of the week, you find yourself with flashlight in hand venturing up to the attic and intuitively pulled to look in the far left corner inside a box you find in an old chest. In there, you find vintage photos of two young women smiling wearing matching lockets. You bring the photos down to show your grandmother what you found and ask who are these women in the photo. She begins to cry as she tells you that she has been missing her deceased sister and praying to her for months to show her a sign that she is still there and loves her. In the photos are your grandmother and her deceased sister.

How to Develop

Before you ever open yourself up to communicating with spirits, you must become very strong in discernment. Master your ability of enforcing psychic protection. Do not use Ouija boards or summon spirits. Only practice developing your mediumship skills once you have established a solid protocol for working within an energetically safe and sacred space. There is no need for fear when developing your mediumship craft, however make it clear to all realms that you are not leaving yourself vulnerable and you are not one to be messed with.

If you are a medium empath, you will naturally develop your skills as you read ahead in this book. Developing your psychic senses such as clairaudience and clairvoyance support your medium empathic skills. Just make sure to always follow the steps of clearing your energy first, grounding, protecting, establishing boundaries, then opening.

If you'd like to practice with like-minded individuals, join a mediumship practice group. Take a course online or read some books on techniques for tapping in to the spirit realm. Learn from other mediums who have established a career in the art form.

Dental Empath

Dental empaths are able to understand information and connect to the dental health of another, even without dental training, all by connecting with the consciousness of the teeth. Yes, the teeth are alive! That is how they have the ability to regenerate, which is a little known fact.

The current model of the dental industry keeps us trapped in a cycle of fear and helpless, promoting that we need regular manufactured care dependent upon a specialist outside of ourselves just to keep our teeth healthy. Considering the amount of sugar and chemicals in the standard person's diet as well as additives to the water (fluoride does nothing to protect the teeth, it only calcifies the pineal gland) and lack of awareness for our own regenerative abilities, this keeps many of us in the dark about dental care.

Strengths
Dental empaths have an inherent knowledge of natural dental healing that has long been hijacked and suppressed by profiting powers. The dental industry as we know it will begin to be phased out as more and more dental empaths come online over time.

Challenges
Most people have a trace amount of this gift. Whenever you clench your jaw or grind your teeth at night, it is due to energy

that you have picked up from other people or not dealing within yourself expressed through the degradation of teeth and jaw. Since mastering the skills of dental empathy have not been made mainstream yet, the energetic information that you receive does not clear away, but rather it remains in your teeth and jaw until it is either interpreted, received, or cleared.

Example
Your friend's elderly mother keeps complaining about throbbing pain in her elbow. She has seen multiple specialists, physical therapists, and has even gone as far as having a surgery to fix it. Yet, after all this effort and expense, she still experiences the chronic pain. You intuitively ask her one afternoon is she has any mercury fillings in her mouth. She shares that she does and they are very old. You strongly suspect these old mercury fillings have something to do with her elbow pain. On a lark, she decides to go to the dentist and have these fillings removed. Once she does, the elbow pain officially resolves itself within the week of removing the fillings.

How to Develop
You may already have an interest or fondness for your teeth. Start to pay attention to them more closely as if they are communicating to you through repetitive presentations, such as a dull throb or a sensory tingle. Observe what you are experiencing as you open up your awareness to your teeth.

Venture out to explore various topics such as teeth reflexology and seek out alternative dental care. Learn as much as you can about what others in the alternative dental community are discovering. By sharing information and resources, you can continue to develop your sensory perceptions and attune to what your teeth, or someone else's teeth, are communicating.

Mechanical Empath

Mechanical empaths can understand intricate processes of machines. By feeling the machine, thinking like a machine, a mechanical empath can have an intimate understanding without having any practical knowledge or education about the machine or technology used by the equipment.

This skillset of mechanical empathy can also extend to computer and electronic technology, as well as artificial intelligence.

Strengths
Mechanical empaths have a knack for fixing broken processes in physical form as well as upgrading current processes to make them better. Efficiency and effectiveness are highly regarded as standards with this skillset.

Mechanical empaths make great machinists, inventors, engineers, ship captains, hardware and software developers, teachers, architects, robotics scientists, and programmers.

Challenges
Mechanical empaths can often be viewed as antisocial or difficult to get close to due to their preference for working with software or machinery. It is much easier to understand the intricacies of a computer problem versus the complexities of human emotion. Interpersonal relationships can be a struggle.

Example

Morse code is the language that connects humans to machinery. Computers use 1s and 0s as its base language. Machinery uses on and off as its base language. Morse code is a series of long tones, short tones and breaks in tone that can be translated to reveal more information. Samuel Morse, one of the people who figured out Morse code, was a mechanical empath who was interested and driven to communicate in a simplified and efficient yet effective manner.

How to Develop

Developing mechanical empathy is fairly easy since achievements in machinery and technology are highly celebrated. In fact, it is quite a competitive arena to develop farther and faster than your adversaries.

For this reason, it is important to remain connected to the heart space and your ties to humanity when developing mechanical empathy. Focus on what can be developed or implemented using your gifts that would benefit humanity as a whole, rather than profiting a select few.

Extraterrestrial Empath

Extraterrestrial empaths, also known as ET empaths or channels, have the ability to connect with beings from alternate dimensions, galaxies, star systems and other realms. Not only communicating with but also channeling these beings such as Angels, Ascended Masters and ETs are the mark of an ET empath. There is a naturally high bandwidth available that supports the ability to connect with groups of ETs and collectives of consciousness as well.

Strengths

ET empaths can connect with and bring through higher dimensional information as well as access a higher vantage point to the human condition. Empowered ET empaths serve as a guiding light during challenging times for humanity as they can facilitate healing transmissions and activating truths for many.

By accessing a greater collective awareness, ET empaths can gain an understanding for current energetic trends and predict probabilities by gauging the current energy climate.

Working with trusted ETs and higher dimensional beings can lead to a fulfilling and elevating life experience for the empath as well. They become friends, trusted allies and offer a higher point of view that can serve as personal support in this human experience.

Challenges

ET empaths can often struggle with feeling as if earth is not home and feel a deep, despondency when witnessing the state of humanity.

Feelings of overwhelm connected to the collective energy can bleed through into every day life, making it hard to focus on simple tasks and responsibilities.

Another challenge is experiencing fear around extraterrestrial contact since there is so much misinformation about universal life. Due to not having the correct information or influences, and not understanding the differences of ET races and motives, uneducated ET empaths can be easily fooled by malevolent ETs.

A good way to tell if you are channeling or listening to a trickster energy being channeled is the 90-10 rule. If 90% of the information shared deeply resonates while 10% feels way off or wrong, be very wary. Always question everything you are hearing or receiving from external entities and hold it against your heart chakra to see if it really feels true to you.

Example

In the recent decades, great strides have been made in the ET empath and channeling community. With familiar names like Esther Hicks channeling Abraham, Darryl Anka channeling Bashar, and even the controversial Barbara Marciniak channeling the Pleiadians, more and more people are becoming familiarized with the phenomenon of channeling — which in the eyes of the ETs themselves, is just a typical method of communication even though it's still amazing to many of us.

How to Develop

Much like when developing your mediumship empath skills, it is important to strengthen your skills of discernment and master protecting your energy before you open up to extraterrestrial life. It is true that many ETs are benevolent, ascended and unconditionally loving. However, the opposite is also true. There are nefarious ETs that you do not want to allow into your energy field. Keep your connection to your extraterrestrial contacts on the frequency of unconditional love only and you can rest assured that you can trust them.

Raising your vibration through out your entire life is an essential step to working with extraterrestrial contacts. Your mission in life also has a lot to do with it. If you feel a strong soul desire to be of service to humanity, work to heal and strengthen yourself in all ways so that you are living a life of love. Be guided by your heart. Anchor Christ consciousness into the earth plane. This increases your chances of clear communication with ascended beings.

Automatic writing is an excellent way to develop your extraterrestrial empath skills. It is often considered an accessible vehicle when you open up your crown chakra and allow the higher guidance and information to channel through you and onto the paper you're writing upon or the screen that you are typing. This is an excellent method to engage in conversational exchange and have your questions answered.

Heyoka Empath

Heyoka empaths are probably one of the most intense types of empaths to be. I call the Heyoka empath "The Healer through Chaos, Destroyer of Egos."

Heyoka is a Lakota term that means "fool" or "sacred clown." Not the most flattering of monikers, but definitely one of the most impactful and influential empath types, whether you like it or not.

Heyokas naturally think, move, behave and express themselves in such radically different ways than what is considered conservative or normal. You go completely against the grain and shake things up just by being naturally free spirited.

Heyokas are a natural-born catalyst for change. You are pure alchemy in human form, here on earth to usher others to their awakening. Again, whether you like it or not.

Strengths

Heyoka empaths are some of the funniest people on earth. By using humor to help facilitate healing (even when unaware that this is what is happening) is such an incredible gift.

Heyoka empaths tend to be really fun people to be around, until you're not. Incredibly creative people with a good judge of character, Heyokas make great artists, entertainers, comedians, satirists, provocateurs, commentators, doctors, healers, and content creators.

Challenges

Heyoka empaths can be viewed as being difficult to deal with or hard to be around. You tend to be outcast or ostriciszed from the group leaving you to feel rejected. Due to the struggles with patience or sharing the stage, so to speak, Heyokas often interrupt people while they're speaking. Dyslexia is also a common struggle for many Heyoka since they view the world in such radically different ways, in this case literally.

It can be a lifelong challenge to stay close to people. You trigger people and put them off so easily yet you deeply care for the health, happiness and wholeness of people. You are deeply caring but can feel very alone in life due to this.

Example

You have a hard time making and maintaining close personal friendships and relationships because you tend to trigger people very easily. You just happen to say the wrong thing at the wrong time for other people who may react in a very negative and aggressive way toward you. You may feel as if you don't understand what you said or did wrong to incite this reaction.

You may feel like you don't deserve such harsh treatment or can't understand why someone doesn't like you.

Little do you know, you said something that directly touched on a hidden wound causing an emotionally charged response to come rushing out of this person. They didn't see it coming and they could't hide their wound from you or even from themself. Essentially, your existence and interaction serves as a mirror reflecting back to the person where they are unhealed.

How to Develop

There isn't much to develop in the ways of a Heyoka aside from developing and empowering oneself as a healthy and stable empath in general. However, embracing the fact that you are a Heyoka is instrumental to your success because it can be a tough go.

Being a Heyoka empath is not an easy role to play in life. You deeply care for people. You enjoy having fun and sharing laughter with others. You feel their emotions so deeply and relate so intimately. Yet your inherent skill of catalyzing spontaneous awakenings and energetic shifts can be so polarizing for those who can't handle it.

Accepting this is a part of your skillset and learning to love that you are making such a profound impact on the souls others will make your position in life much easier to deal with and ultimately more satisfying for you.

WEEK 8

INTUITION – HOW AN EMPATH RECEIVES ENERGY

Empath's are defined as one who psychically understands the state of another person, place or thing.

> *A person with extra-sensoryempathic ability, capable of sensing the emotions of others around them in a way unexplained by conventional science and psychology.*
> (Src: wordnik.com)

For years, psychic abilities have been touted as unattainable, magical powers that only a select chosen few in this world have. There was no mainstream discussion about how to develop these abilities because either you're born with it or you're not. You better leave it to the professionals.

Even those that were born with it, there is still a lot of fear and misunderstanding surrounding psychics and psychic abilities, often regarded as only being connected to practicing dark arts. Being an empath has seriously gotten some bad press with a whole lot of misinformation transmitted around it. Need I bring up the Salem Witch Trials?

Well, I'm here to tell you that having psychic abilities is not a curse, it's not a paranormal phenomenon and it's not as out of reach as many want you to believe. We are all able to connect with Source energy to receive information and guidance. In order to do so, we all came prewired with the ability to connect to Universal consciousness, Divine love. We just haven't quite mastered the technology yet.

This point in time is an era of awakening. Of many individuals waking up to the truth that they are somehow able to sense things, know things, connect with things without any sensible or scientifically explainable reason. Enter: Intuition

Everything in this world is energy. Everything! Empaths are simply receiving and perceiving energetic information due to a highly sensitive intuition. The unmanaged empath is being bombarded by energetic information like a log caught in a raging river. The energetic information just washes over them and pummels them.

Yet the empowered empath can focus and attune the powerful intuition to translate and understand the energetic information, or even disregard it if necessary. This can be enhanced by receiving psychic information, messages of communication from your spirit guides and receiving clearly defined information, downloads and insights.

Receiving this information is useless unless you trust yourself and your own intuition, which is why one of the major defining differences between and unmanaged empath and empowered empath is the empowered empath trusts their intuition over everything else.

How many times has something occurred to you only to brush it off and then later it turned out to be true? When your instinct is validated, you're getting the clear message to trust yourself and pay attention to those original thoughts!

Doubt is a lower frequency emotion. Keep your vibe high and practice trusting the information you receive without questioning it and watch what happens.

Also, to better understand an empath and how you receive energy, it's important to discuss spirit guides, soul origin and past lives.

Step 1: What is a Spirit Guide?

In my experience, spirit guides are whatever you need them to be. They can be spirit animals, deceased loved ones, guardian angels, ancient ancestors, a collective of extra terrestrials, aspects of your own higher mind, an ascended master such as Jesus or Quan Yin, earth spirits or even dragons. Spirit guides show up in our lives in a form that we are most open to and will fully embrace in order to be open to their guidance, support and love.

Religious programming or past indoctrination can have a lot to do with how they show up, as well. For example, if you were brought up to fear anything that is not considered "holy," your spirit guide may show up as Jesus or an Arch Angel. Or if you still hold a distrust for any sort of man-made religion yet you believe in the power of nature, your spirit guides may show up as fairies or tree spirits. Or if you have always felt like you came here from another star system, your guides may appear as an intergalactic committee relaying off world intel. Conversely, if you don't trust any metaphysical being beyond yourself, your spirit guide can be your own Higher self or show up as an aspect or extension of yourself. Your spirit guide can even be your own inner child if you are working through some lessons regarding your own innocence and restoring your purity.

The truth is that your spirit guides show up as you need them and when you are ready for them. You will have many, many, many different guides and guardians along your path as there are millions of beings that love and support you unconditionally.

They are aware of and considerate to what you are ready for so you are not overwhelmed or shut down from fear or explode with ego. They also abide by Universal law and never intervene against your free will.

A truly loving and trustworthy spirit guide will never try to persuade you, manipulate you or infer upon your freedom of experience. When you are ready, they trust you to invite them into your heart. You ask for the help. You open yourself up to developing a loving and trusting bond with them. You are the one who initiates the relationship. It is all up to you!

You may go through lessons of discernment as you learn what guidance is from a trusted spirit guide and what messages are coming from opportunistic negative energies interfering with your signal. This is why it is so important you learn about reading your own vibration and setting boundaries before opening up to other worlds. It's the difference between being a naive tourist and a seasoned traveler in a foreign land. You know the game and have become well educated in self protection so you don't fall for any spiritual three-card monte or anything else that doesn't serve you.

Until you are ready, just know that you will never be without love or protection on your journey. You are never truly alone. You are too precious and your spirit guides are always here, cheering you on from the sidelines. They genuinely want to see you succeed! They are your biggest cheerleaders in life.

The relationship you have with your spirit guides is mutually beneficial, as well. Imagine you are a new recruit at Planet Boot Camp with big dreams to climb the ranks and ascend your consciousness. You are selected to be the first recruit to run the obstacle course. As someone who naturally aspires to be team captain someday, once you complete your run and successfully circumvent life challenges, you naturally turn back to guide the others through the same obstacles you just overcame. You understand that they may respond differently to each task than you did but you are patient and believe in them because you went through the same difficulty and found success. This is what it's like for your spirit guides!

You, the human incarnate, are receiving higher wisdom and guidance from your spirit guide because they've been through it before. The spirit guide is expanding their understanding by holding a higher perspective and nurturing the evolution of your consciousness. It's truly a win-win for all!

Step 2: What are my Past Lives and Soul Origin?

You have lived many, many, many lifetimes and not all of these lives were on planet earth. You have been many things, many different people and have lived in many different worlds. You have played many different roles, been many races, religions and even different genders. You have lived lives as different species. You have had all kinds of bodies, human-form and otherwise. You are an old soul who has seen and been through quite a lot!

All of these experiences that you have been through are documented in your Akashic Records — the records of everything that ever was and everything that ever will be. Your lifetime as a conscious light form living in the angelic realm is recorded there. Your lifetime as a single-celled organism living on a desolate planet in another galaxy is recorded there. Your lifetime where you died a horrible, tragic death too early is recorded there. The lifetime filled with peace where you lived a long and healthy span of 750 years is recorded there. And the lifetime you are living now is also being recorded there.

Every life experience your consciousness has ever gone through in the history of your soul's journey is recorded like a never ending tape recorder. This tape holds record of every lesson you have learned, every challenge you have overcome, every pain you have suffered, every bit of love you have shared, every victory you have achieved, every wrinkle in the history of time that you have experienced, it is all there.

As you can imagine, sometimes healing work needs to be done regarding any past life trauma causing repeating issues in your current lifetime. At the same time, you have a wealth of information literally imprinted onto the record of your soul that you can access any time. When we talk about soul wisdom, it is not something to be underestimated because it took a lot to get here.

You have done all things and been all things and have the capability to tap into the vein of Universal consciousness. As I mentioned in Week 1, you can retrieve information as it is all available to you. As helpful and irreplaceable as spirit guides are, they are here to help remind you of the infinitely powerful being you are. The truth is that you are capable of tapping in and tuning in all on your own. Just like you are capable of using the internet to search anything you like, Universal consciousness is just like that, except there's no censorship.

You may experience different approaches to the same lesson over and over again in the same lifetime, which ultimately is more information ammo for your arsenal = wisdom. This is the repetition of emotional patterns and karmic cycles. Then, once you leave the physical plane just like your spirit guides, you will eventually be given an option to work with a human incarnate to guide them through their version of the very same lesson and challenges, but to be experienced and navigated in a whole new perspective.

Though you have lived many different lifetimes living in various bodies, learning different lessons and experiencing different worlds, there are a few select lifetimes that carry a lot of influence over your current lifetime. These lifetimes may have involved intensive training and mastery of abilities and knowledge in order to bring forth during your current lifetime. These lifetimes may also influence a karmic weight that you have been working through in this lifetime. These key lifetimes can be considered your **soul origin**.

For example, you spent 3 lifetimes in Atlantis as an oracle forecasting future events and gazing into the time horizon but no one heeded your cautionary warnings about the events that would end in devastation. These lifetimes greatly influence your clairvoyant abilities in this life where you may have been gifted from birth but felt insecure to share your gift with others for fear of not being believed.

Another example I have been seeing more and more of in the recent years are children being born who have spent centuries in higher dimensions just to train for being in a lower dimension on earth during the transition into a new age. This world is not for the faint of heart and we need highly evolved souls who know how to survive something as big as this global shift. These rainbow children coming in have highly attuned consciousness and will be and do great things for humanity's evolution.

If you're interested in tapping into your own past lives and learning more about your soul's experiences, gifts and wisdom, here are a few avenues to explore that will help you dive deeper:

- Akashic records reading by a professional intuitive
- Past life regression therapy
- QHHT session by certified practitioner
- Shamanic journeys with a trusted shaman
- Guided meditation for past life
- Crystal journeys

Reading List!

I offer a digital booklet and crystal starter kit in my shop (ProjectEmpath.com > Shop) specifically designed to give you the direction and prompts to delve into past lives through crystal journeys:

1. Empowered Empath Journey Journal, Kate Moriah Kyser.

Step 3: Develop The Clairs

The clairs are the sensory vehicles in which you psychically receive and process energetic information. They are the channels in which you communicate with your environment and spirit guides. Clair, the French word for clear, indicates a clear intuitive sense or sensory channel.

There are a number of different clairs that you can develop. You may already have a few that are operational or "turned on" right now. One may be stronger than another but others can be developed and enhanced. Just like working a muscle at a gym over time to strengthen it, you can strengthen your psychic senses with a little bit of time and focused practice.

Clairempathy

Definition
Intuitive feeling, clear emotion, clear feeling of passion and suffering

Symptoms

Sensing or feeling information that has not been directly shared, knowing things without being told, refer to Week 1: Identify

How to Develop

- Step out of your head and into senses
- Spend a week eating very rich, colorful foods that are appealing to all the senses
- Doodle while your focus wanders not paying attention to what your pen is doing but rather what you are bringing through you
- Do a detox to clear your channel
- Cross your senses — visualize music, smell colors, listen to your body
- Read or sense the vibes of strangers in a public space based on what you are seeing and noticing
- Volunteer and be of service
- Do something for the greater good to tap into the soul desire to shine your light — this opens you up as you operate within the heart space and gives to the universe opening you up to then receive from others
- Honor the purge — as an empath you will go through cycles of rest which is needed as a part of you clearing your energy regularly

Crystals to Work With

Any crystals are great for an empath to work with, especially when you have a conscious intention. However, when developing your gifts of empathy, here are a few to start working with:

- Selenite
- Angel Aura Quartz
- Chrysanthemum Stone
- Angelite
- Black Tourmaline
- Smokey Quartz
- Black Obsidian
- Citrine
- Rose Quartz

Clairvoyance

Definition
The psychic ability of clear seeing, intuitive vision, acute intuitive insight or perception

Symptoms
Flashes of light or color, oracle visions, active daydreamer, vivid dreams, visual images in mind's eye, colorful imagination, catching light or movement out of the corner of your eye, solid sense of direction, able to visualize easily, appreciate visual beauty, can see auras

How to Develop
- Work with 3rd eye chakra
- Decalcify pineal gland by quitting fluoride toothpaste and stop drinking unfiltered tap water
- Detox from chloride and calcium which hardens the pineal gland
- Visualization games that involve color and movement — such as imagining a pink elephant walking across

a ballroom who is trying different pieces of cake with various icing on it
- Card and memory games like word search, memory search, magic eye or treasure hunt
- Telepathic games like "I spy" where someone holds an image in their mind's eye and you attempt to connect with what they are seeing

Crystals to Work With
- Iolite
- Clear Quartz
- Labradorite
- Larimar
- Celestite

Claircognisance

Definition
Intuitive knowing, the psychic ability to receive knowledge without being given the information directly

Symptoms
Good judge of character, spend a lot of time thinking, precognition, often have instant ideas, helpful thoughts or solutions, can find lost items or people easily, love for learning, takes risks based on gut feeling which are usually right, human lie detector, can clearly see the outcome to situations

How to Develop
- Cleanse and open the crown chakra
- Automatic writing
- Practice trusting your first thought and going with it

- Clear the mind through meditation
- Work with Zener cards
- Play with a deck of cards face down and predict the color or suit of the next card before you flip it over

Crystals to Work With
- Sodalite
- Fluorite
- Labradorite
- Sapphire
- Lapis Lazuli

Clairsentience

Definition
Intuitive knowing by feeling, sensing and experiencing in the physical body

Symptoms
Chills, body sensations, phantom pains, feeling ill around certain people or places, experiencing seemingly random tightness or pressure in throat, head or body, you feel heavy or light depending on what you are interacting with or surrounded by, feeling tingles or light touches when no one is near you

How to Develop
- Clear your touch senses by removing overstimulation — no scratchy fabrics or uncomfortable clothing, ask for some space from your family if necessary
- Open energy channels such as getting accupuncture, accupressure, or Reiki to open up your sensory circuitry

- Practice what your body senses around you by closing your eyes and walk down a hallway (without stairs or obstacles) and sense your way forward
- Do a spiritual touch meditation where you call in your spiritual team and ask them to touch you
- Play an energy game with a partner — have them stand in another room and touch a part of their own body then try to guess what they are touching by tuning in to where you are feeling pressure or warmth on your body
- Play psychometry games — try touching random objects that belong to other people and see what you feel in your body, ask if your intuition is right on

Crystals to Work With
- Blue Tourmaline
- Petalite
- Dumorterite
- Moldavite
- Clear Topaz

Clairaudience

Definition
Intuitive audio, psychic hearing, the ability to hear sounds outside of the normal range of perception

Symptoms
Sensitive to loud sounds and sudden noises, hearing popping noises in ears, crackling noises, static or high pitched tones, being musically inclined, hearing disembodied voices, inclination to talk to oneself, you can get a feeling

for a person just by hearing their name or voice, enjoying or needing quiet

How to Develop
- Clear your channel and purify your antenna by paying attention to what you're listening to, remove low vibration music and toxic entertainment from your life
- Heal any trauma and cut cords from anyone who was hurtful in your past as this may lead to hearing a negative voice in your head
- Sit in silence often
- Meditate and isolate the different voices within you — ego is the loudest, instinct is the next voice once we move past ego, the quietest voice is your intuition
- Do "The Orchestra Exercise" — Observe all of the noises within your environment and listen to them all together like an orchestra, then one by one begin to isolate the noises separately to identify each individual source of noise
- Talk to your guides and have conversations with them — see what you can hear in response
- Put on a random music playlist and see what lyrics catch your attention with pertinent messages for you
- Listen to binaural beats to quiet your mind chatter and hear your own inner dialogue
- Making various sounds and noises with your mouth and feel into the different vibrations you feel through out your head and body, this may feel weird at first but you are opening different frequencies so play with it and see how it feels

Crystals to Work With
- Phantom Quartz
- Sapphire
- Angel Wing Selenite
- Fulgurite
- Herderite

Clairgustance

Definition
Intuitive taste, the ability to taste something that is not literally in your mouth

Symptoms
Having a finely tuned palette where you can taste subtle flavors, may not be able to handle spicy food, experiencing a mouth-feel for something without actually putting it in your mouth, may be sensitive to certain food textures or have aversions to certain foods due to texture

How to Develop
- Clear and rest your senses by quitting overly stimulating chemicals, toxins or overly processed foods
- Do a palette test with a partner or your family — feed each other where you guess what you're tasting without peeking
- Conjure taste through thought — look at pictures of food and tune into the flavors
- Play a taste test energy game where you are on the phone with a loved one and have them drink or eat something and see if you are able to tap into what they are ingesting

Crystals to Work With
- Clear Quartz
- Labradorite
- Lapis Lazuli
- Kyanite
- Chrysocolla

Clairalience, Clairscent, Clairsentency

Definition
Clear smelling, psychic scent, intuitive smell

Symptoms
Having a strong sense of smell like a hound's nose, you smell things before other people do, smelling scents that are not there

How to Develop

- Cleanse and expand root and throat chakra as this sense connects there
- Strengthen sense of smell by doing things like quitting smoking cigarettes or pipe tobacco, stop over seasoning food or using extremely hot seasoning
- Sniff test everything including things that normally don't have a smell like a crystal or a piece of paper
- Take in the scent of anything you can — this allows you to create a catalog of information
- Sniff test photos — search images online and imagine the scents connected to the photo like a basket of fruit or a scene at the beach
- Work with essential oils

- Journal your emotional response to various scents and dive into how these scents make you feel, what emotions do these scents evoke within you?

Crystals to Work With

- Bloodstone
- Carnelian
- Herkimer Diamond
- Kyanite
- Snowflake Obsidian

Clairtangency, Clairtaction, Psychometry

Definition
Intuitive touch, psychic touch, the ability to receive information by touching a person, place, animal or object

Symptoms
Feeling overwhelmed in cluttered places as too much energy to process, naturally good at giving massage, hands just know where to go and how much pressure to apply, been told you "feel" good or others like touching you, thrift stores or pawn shops make you feel gross, have a tendency to give things away or pass items along because it just "feels" right, have a tendency to keep your space, self and items clean

How to Develop
- Host a psychometry party where friends bring various objects and you must guess who brought it and the story behind it

- Play with different crystals or herbs — hold each one and write down all impressions you get or the healing properties they offer, you may just discover that you're a plant or crystal empath
- Pet animals (with the owner's permission) and see if you can get a feel for the animal's personality, habits and preferences
- Practice massaging or transferring healing light intentions to your partner, let your hands guide you and have their response validate the wisdom in your hands

Crystals to Work With

This is another time when you can literally use any crystal that calls to you and use it to help you develop. However, if your intention is specifically to enhance your psychic gift of clairtangency, here are some options:

- Clear Quartz
- Nuummite
- Serpentine
- Golden Healer Quartz
- Moldavite

Dream Walking, Dream Worker, Dreamweaver

Definition

The ability to retrieve information in the dream world, a lucid dreamer, one who takes active control over the direction of their dreams, one who visits and connects with others in dreams

Symptoms

Sleep paralysis, astral travel without trying, lucid dreamer, vivid dreams, wake up with solutions to problems you had the night before, graphic or detailed dreams, being told often you were in someone else's dreams, appearing in many people's dreams, dreaming about events before they happen, vivid dream recall

How to Develop

- Water exercise — drink a glass of water before bed in order to prompt dreams of urination which ultimately trigger lucidity
- Keep a dream journal to write down and interpret any messages or symbols you remember from your dreams
- Write down a question you may have for your Higher self or spirit guide right before you go to sleep, write down the answer upon waking
- Talk to the person or people that appear in your dreams and see if there are any connections or telepathic exchange happening
- Meditate right before going to sleep and invite your spirit guide to meet you in your dream
- If you notice a clock in your dream, pay attention to the time, or if you notice a mirror in the dream, look in the mirror — these practices will reconnect you with your conscious will so you are better able to control your dream
- Listen to a lucid dreaming hypnosis before going to sleep

Crystals to Work With

- Herkimer Diamond
- Amethyst
- Moonstone
- Dream Quartz
- Azurite

INTERPLAY –
DEVELOP A LANGUAGE

When you first begin to expand your awareness and communicate with energy, it's an exciting but foreign new world! The more you tap in and communicate with various energy such as spirit guides, animals, plants, crystals, even your own higher self, over time you will develop a language that is personal to your interpretation or understanding of the information.

Step 1: Follow the Golden Nuggets

When you are first expanding your awareness of incoming messages from spirit and establishing a language to communicate with the energy, it can be a bit confusing as to what you are seeing and experiencing or how to accurately interpret the messages that are coming in. If you are extremely unfamiliar with this practice or don't have the proper support or teachers though out your life to guide you to embrace and develop your abilities, it can be downright scary.

Many children who are born with their psychic gifts turned on in full force will shut down their abilities early due to not understanding what they are experiencing. Chances are you were one of those children!

This is why I always recommend to begin communicating with spirit by listening to your own energetic feedback first. Follow the bread crumbs of desire. I call these "golden nuggets of intuition." Let me explain.

Often true desires can be repressed and stuffed deep within our shadow self because we are taught in some way that our desires are not natural or correct or acceptable or normal or even possible. But these little nuggets of excitement that you feel rise up within you are usually messages themselves.

If you allow yourself to honestly observe when something interests you, makes you feel curious or gives you a feeling of excitement, no matter how unfamiliar or out of reach it may seem, it will lead you to uncovering more information that your soul is searching for. It will also lead you to another golden nugget of intuition beyond that.

A good indicator of these golden nuggets is a feeling I call "nervouscited." It's when you are considering something that makes you feel somewhat nervous or hesitant to move forward but you can't deny that this excites you on some level. Basically, you feel nervous and excited at the same time. This is guidance straight from your higher self in an attempt to get you to break free from any resistance to your own soul growth and development.

Nervous + Excited = "Nervouscited" = guidance you can trust!

You are encouraged to follow each golden nugget to discover where that trail of desire is leading you. You will always be lead exactly where you need to go or what you need to do in order to reveal more and more and more of what is aligned for your soul.

Sometimes when you follow these golden nuggets, you are lead to a past trauma or wound that needs to be healed and released so that you can move forward more freely in your life. Sometimes you are lead to an opportunity to advance to the next stage of your life and spiritual growth! Most times, you stumble upon a blessing that you wouldn't have found unless you truly listened to your intuition.

Either way, desire (the true desire that comes from deep within your heart-of-hearts, and not a surface desire like addiction) is always going to lead you closer to your best, most powerful self!

Step 2: Pay Attention to the Symbols

Your spiritual team is always well aware of your current state. This includes your readiness, willingness and availability to receive messages. Are you in a state of 'no' or a state of 'yes?'

If you are existing in a state of fear, it is much more difficult (sometimes impossible) to get a message through to you if you're closed off to receiving it. Yet, if you are making the effort and setting the intention consistently to remain open, you're more likely to develop a relationship and open channels of communication with your team!

Having said that, it is imperative that you always clear your energy and set an intention of protection before opening yourself up to communicate directly with any spirit, energy or being outside of yourself. Remember, you are not protecting yourself out of fear but rather from a place of personal power.

Once you set your intention of protection and sovereignty in your spiritual exchange, play with a wide range of methods to ultimately develop your personal language with your team.

The following are some ways in which spirit will communicate with you:

Repetition — if you notice repeating numbers, patterns, names, places, colors, you keep bumping into the same person or anything that stands out to you frequently, take note of what is trying to catch your attention.

What are some things that have been repeatedly getting your attention lately?

_____

_____

_____

Journal — you can communicate directly with your spiritual team through journaling. Direct your focus to your intended guide, ask a question, and allow whatever information wants to come through you to channel through you. Trust what is coming through. The moment you doubt or question your connection, you interrupt the stream of consciousness and may disrupt the connection.

What is a question that you can bring to your journal time?

_____

_____

_____

Synchronicities — when you notice something lining up perfectly, making you wonder what are the chances of this working out so synchronized and harmoniously, take note that your guidance has had a helping hand in allowing certain events to unfold so you may get the information or resources that you need.

What is something that has occurred in your life recently that feels divinely orchestrated?

_____

_____

_____

Angel Numbers — the repeating number patterns often appear in synchronized ways where your spiritual team is conveying information and energy codes through the vibration of numbers. Everything in this world is energy and numbers hold their own specialized frequencies. If you notice a reoccurring number pattern in your life, there are numerous resources online where you can search various interpretations of these number codes to help you out. You are also free to determine your own meaning for yourself.

What number has significance for you or has been reoccurring in your awareness?

_____

_____

_____

Triggers — your own memories and life experiences serve as a reference point of information for you that your spiritual team may use to bring information to your awareness. For example, there is wisdom that you glean only from living through a life experience. You may be triggered or reminded of your past when encountering a new person in order to warn you that this person carries similar energy to your past painful experience. You may not have known why this person felt "off" to you and may have possibly ignored this cautionary sense if you did not have that triggered memory of an experience that you know all too well and don't want to repeat.

What is something that has triggered a memory or emotional response for your recently and what did you feel?

_____

_____

_____

Signs — these can come in many forms such as finding feathers or dimes from your angels, to overhearing a conversation that answers a question you've carried in your heart. Signs can also be much more attention grabbing such as something falling loudly in an empty room or glass breaking when no one is around to cause that.

What was a sign that you received recently from your angels?

_____

_____

_____

Animals — all birds, animals and insects are messengers. Animals can appear to you in your dreams, in your daily life, show up as symbolism or even visit you directly just to get your attention where you can't *not* notice them. If you find that an animal, bird or insect is showing up in your life frequently, it may have a message for you. There are numerous resources online to search for animal spirit message meanings.

Has there been an animal, bird or insect popping up in your awareness recently? What is their message for you?

_____

_____

_____

Journeying — doing journey work, such as shamanic journeys, past life regressions, crystal journeys or plant medicine work can introduce you to a guide or aspect of yourself that is ready to communicate. By entering into an altered state, your usual defenses of rational mind and 3D fear programming are lowered, making it easier to communicate directly with your consciousness.

What type of journey work would you be interested in exploring more?

_____

_____

_____

_____

Strangers — seemingly random interactions with people you don't know may not be as random as you think since strangers are often used as a vehicle for spirit to communicate with you directly. If you've ever had someone come up to you and say something that just stayed with you or gave you chills, this is an example of your spirit team talking to you through them. Be aware that opportunistic energies can do the same thing, so if you have someone approaching you in a chaotic manner, steer clear of them and shield your energy.

What is something random that happened to you recently that stuck with you?

_____

_____

_____

Spiritual Tools — Oracle cards, using a pendulum, muscle testing, water scrying, reading tea leaves and channeling light language are just a few examples of spiritual tools you can use to communicate directly with your guides. These tools are not essential to you communicating but can often provide new and fun ways of receiving messages.

Which spiritual tools have you been curious to explore?

_____

_____

_____

Dreams and Prophecies — guidance will often come to you in dreams or prophetic visions when your logical mind is at rest. During waking life, there is much that demands your cognitive mind to be engaged which often acts as a defense to protect itself. Unfortunately this also means the brain resists higher guidance. When in a dream or meditative state where your mind is at rest, messages and information are better able to come into your consciousness.

Have you had any reoccurring or significantly memorable dreams?

_____

_____

_____

When communicating with you, your spiritual team will usually find the path of least resistance and use the easiest means of communication possible, such as repetition and memory association, when you're open to it.

– Personal Share –

When I was a kid, I really enjoyed cartoons and loved illustrating my own characters. So now, when I receive clairvoyant images in cartoon form during a reading, I know that I am speaking with the energy of a child. This also applies in my personal meditation because for me, cartoon images are a symbol that my inner child is talking. So whenever I have visions or memories of cartoons, the association is already defined between me and my higher guidance that I am not only receiving the information but I also know where it is coming from. I instantly know who I'm communicating with thanks to the predetermined association.

As an extension of this concept, I've shared this example with my husband, how I interpret cartoon images in my mind's eye. He now uses the same understanding when he has cartoon images appear in his mind's eye. Now he has the same association where he identifies it as coming from his own inner child, and so that is what his guidance uses because he has already cognitively accepted and embraced this understanding. It now serves as an easy path of communication for his spiritual team, as well.

— — —

The language that you develop with your spiritual team is a personal process. Symbols that may mean one thing for you may represent something completely different to someone else because their guides are also using the easiest means of understanding, repetition and association.

You may decide over time that for you a dragonfly represents the part of you that travels in between worlds and may bring a message of higher information, whereas another person may see a dragonfly and feel it is a visit from their deceased loved one. It all depends on the spiritual association and language developed to achieve a higher level of spiritual understanding.

There is literally no wrong way to interpret these messages as long as you are paying attention!

Just remember this is a relationship you are developing with your spiritual team. It is a balanced and equal energy exchange. Getting into the habit of blindly following symbolic prompts can be a disempowering practice. If you ever find yourself saying "because spirit told me to do it," then it is time for you to reclaim your authority over your own will.

It's important to remain aware of how YOU are feeling and resonating when you interact with these prompts, messages and symbols from spirit. If it doesn't resonate, don't try to make it fit. Take what resonates and leave the rest behind.

Congratulations!! Look at You Go!

Congratulations! You have finished the Empowered Empath! Your own personal journey learning how to go from anxious to empowered is now complete.

You've learned how to:

1. Identify — What is am Empath?
2. Illuminate — The Unmanaged Empath
3. Influence — Establish a Sanctuary
4. Ignite — Chakras, Raising Vibration
5. Implant — Grounding
6. Insulate — Protection, Shielding, Boundaries
7. Integrate — Types of Empaths

8. Intuition — The Clairs

9. Interplay — Develop a Language

At this point, you now have an entire spiritual tool kit chock full of knowledge and tools to manage your own energy and develop your intuitive craft. You also have this book to reference at any point you need a reminder of how fantastically capable you really are.

If you'd like to continue your empath education, you may be interested in my next book *The Master Empath: Turning Sensitivities into Mastery*. To be notified of upcoming releases and pertinent empath information, subscribe to my newsletter on ProjectEmpath.com

Like a top-of-the-line bicycle, you can go anywhere you want to, as long as you are prepared to be the power behind it. Life isn't obligated to bring you happiness. All life gives you is time. If you want a life filled with all the things that bring you joy, that part is up to you. Good thing you're a powerful creator in touch with your personal power and can make it all happen for yourself!

You already and always have all the answers within yourself. You are an age-old soul who carries wisdom beyond measure. You have a radiant light within you that is just bursting at the seams to shine in this world! You are now ready. Well done!

Happy healing, empowerment and freedom, my friend!

KATE MORIAH

Kate Moriah is a master empath, professional psychic channel and energy-healing practitioner.

Through intuitively reading of energy and tapping into the Akashic Records, she is able to help identify the soul's purpose and unique gifts. Using empathic abilities and shamanic practices, Kate detects and addresses obstacles that may be hindering one's peace of mind and personal expansion.

After meeting with Kate, clients report gaining life-changing insights, positive shifts in their work, relationships and experience an overall sense of well-being and improved quality of life.

Using her gifts such as crystal empathy, intellectual empathy, emotional empathy, animal empathy, clairvoyance, clairsentience, clairaudience, and humor to name a few, Kate's life's work and dedication to the planet is to inspire, encourage, support, and help others heal. She is a safe and trusted resource for personal healing, growth, and well being.

Kate has shared her experiences and wisdoms on radio, public appearances, social media as well as co-authored *Navigating the Clickety Clack* with Jack Canfield and Christy Whitman.

She has also worked with a vast clientele from all over the world, helping people connect with deceased loved ones, removing blockages within their lives, clearing away negative energy and guiding them to build their ideal life.

As an ordained Minister with a degree from the University of Washington in Communications, and Doctor of Divinity from ULC, communicating with everyone from the living to the departed, children, animals, crystals and plants, and everything in between has come naturally since birth.

Kate lives with her daughter in Washington, USA.

Printed in Great Britain
by Amazon

26572693R00126